Memoirs of
a Welshman

by Lyn Clarke

Clarke Books
Anna Maria, Florida

Also by Lyn Clarke:
Ramblings of a Welshman
Reflections of a Welshman

Clarke Books

Published by The TRIAD Publishing Group
Previously published by Peppertree Press under ISBN: 978-1-934246-07-8 &
The TRIAD Publishing Group under ISBN: 978-0-9798244-9-4

ISBN 13: 9781440439797
ISBN 10: 1440439796
Library of Congress Number: 2006932895
Printed in the U.S.A.
Printed October 2008

Memoirs of
a Welshman

An Introduction

It has occurred to me recently that, over the years, I have been involved in so many different areas of work, sport, music, and life in general, that many of the wonderful people associated with me in one sphere of my life know absolutely nothing about the other spheres. The main reason for this lack of cross-pollination is the fact that I have not spent all my time in one place. I've also been influenced, in different ways, by the multi-talented people I've met as I've progressed through life.

I was born in Pontypool in the (then) county of Monmouthshire (South Wales), where I was raised and educated until I was nineteen years of age. Through my work, I moved to the Wirral area of Cheshire (England) and lived, married, had children, and worked there until the age of thirty-six. Another job-related move took me to Michigan in the United States, where I finished the rest of my work career before delicately maneuvering my final move to the wonderful state of Florida where I put pen to paper this very day.

Except for the first of these moves, which was gifted to me, all the others were meticulously devised and deliberately orchestrated by yours truly for the personal gratification of my desire to seek new horizons and to experience different lifestyles. I make no apologies to any of my past employers for using them as a vehicle to achieve the life I chose. I only apologize to the friends and loved ones that I left behind, and to these I say that, in some instances, I have missed them dearly. Some of these people have given me guidance and have nurtured me through my many life changes.

The most influential of these was my late mother Elizabeth Clarke (née Herbert) who above all else taught me two important things: the first was to never commit to something unless you intend to follow it through; the second was that when the going gets tough, the tough get going. She never had much in life, but she soldiered on through all adversities; she never explained and never complained.

Why are you writing all this now, you may ask. Because finally all the pieces of my mosaic life have come together, and, on reflection, only now can I completely appreciate what a wonderful life I have been blessed with. My journey, from the industrial streets of South Wales to a picture-perfect paradise island in the Gulf of Mexico, has been a monumental one — —one that has had many more ups than downs, and one that has been richly enhanced by some of the absolutely best people that any human being could wish to meet in one lifetime. I only wish that I could live it all again so that the second time I could savor each moment and relish each occasion more fully.

I will honor many people throughout this collection of stories, but I want to mention a few right now as being lifelong mentors. First, my rugby captain at Abersychan Technical College, John Harris, who convinced me to play rugby at the age of eleven. This caused me to enjoy the sport, which I fell in love with and played for twenty-five years. Second, the late Mr. Wilf Ivory, my apprentice supervisor, at Girling Ltd., who not only acted as my surrogate father, but also gave me my first big break in life — — the move to Cheshire.

Thirdly, Bobby Harrison, who persuaded me, at the

age of thirty-six, to take up soccer (football) and thus enabled me to remain active for another twenty-five years. Last, my family: my wife, Sharon, who has given me endless encouragement and affection in my later years, and my children, Louise and Richard, who have made me immensely proud by each following his or her chosen career. Each has become a successful professional with a minimal amount of assistance from me. I admire them for who they are and for what they have achieved. I consider myself fortunate to have made so many friends in one lifetime.

One
The Awakening

Why is it that the most bizarre happenings stick in your memory so vividly? Playing street rugby with Billy Lewis, John Pope, Terry Vaux, and all the King Street gang is one such incident. How we played on a street only thirty feet wide was quite astonishing. All of us kids "dummying," side-stepping, and even doing scissor movements in such a restricted space must have augured well in later life when we were let loose on a rugby field about seventy yards wide.

Could street rugby be the reason that Wales produced so many skillful ball handlers back then? I am sure that playing on the streets instead of watching television, as in later times, might have kept Welsh rugby on top for around thirty years.

These games were almost a daily event during the summer school break, but the other big social gathering was the soccer (football) games, which were held on the playing field in back of George Street School. Occasionally the police would chase us kids off, because the school was officially closed for the summer and the school gates locked.

I remember John "Digger" Stanley, a boy five years my senior, kicking me extremely hard on the front left shinbone, from which I carry a notch to this day. He carried me home to my mother and apologized unreservedly about twenty times as he thought he'd broken my leg. I remember John Cross shooting me in my right leg with an arrow from a five-foot, real longbow. Luckily, the tip was dulled for target practice, but it still put an ugly indentation in the back of my calf. Again I was carried home, and John begged my mother not to mention the incident to his mother, otherwise his new bow would be confiscated.

There were only two ways to get into the school field: through the bars of the surrounding railings——if you were small enough--or over the top of the seven-foot high railings——if you were brave enough. The second way in, however, should not be tried on a rainy day, as Brian Waters will confirm. One wet day, he slipped and found himself impaled with a spiked bar through his thigh. He had to be literally lifted off and rushed to hospital.

On another occasion, the police came to my house to investigate a report that Lyn Clarke had forced the iron bars apart to let the neighborhood children in to play soccer. As soon as I confronted Police Constable Window——I was age ten and weighed around seventy pounds——the policemen laughed so hard he almost wet himself. The investigation was closed from that moment.

I also knocked my front teeth through my lower lip when jumping off George Street School nursery building with David Roberts. The roof was flat, and I jumped off without checking where the cement path was located. When I overstretched to reach the grass verge, my head came down on my knees. Yes, I still have that scar, too! I am sure that by the time school started back up in the autumn our parents heaved a collective sigh of relief as King Street had seen its fair share of ambulances during the summer months.

Another memory is of Ray Prosser, our town's rugby-playing hero, arriving by van to visit his pal, John "Fuzzy" Emmett, who lived directly across the street from my mother's house on King Street. When leaving, Ray's van would never start, so about a dozen of the King Street gang, boys and girls, would push it over to Conway Road.On the downhill slope, Ray would jump the clutch as the van gathered momentum on its way toward town. Ray went on to play for Wales and the British Lions, and Fuzzy left town to play rugby league for the Rochdale Hornets. We kids never saw Fuzzy again.

One day my mother sent me over to lend Mrs. Emmett a stick of butter. John had not yet gone north and was sitting in a tin bath in front of the fire having just come off shift from Tyr Pentis coal mine. I couldn't help but notice he had a long scar on his back. It ran from his left shoulder diagonally down to his right hip. Later I asked my mother how this had happened, and she told me that during a rock fall at the coal mine John had been pinned underneath, but he was so strong that he'd arched his back, and six other miners were able to crawl out through the space he'd made. John was never given any bravery award for this selfless act.

I remember watching, as a young boy and from my classroom window at Abersychan Tech, Malcolm Price practicing rugby. I was mesmerized; I had never seen anyone move so smoothly and quickly while changing direction at the same time. I remember wishing that my sister Ann (Bunny) would marry Malcolm Price. Had it happened, I would have been as proud as a peacock, because Malcolm went on to play for the Royal Air Force, Wales, and the British Lions. He then changed codes and went on to play for Leeds and Great Britain rugby league teams. His touchdown (try) for Wales against Scotland at Cardiff, when he made a looping outside break between the center and the wing, without a finger being laid on him, must go down in my memory as one of the best individual scores that I've ever seen! His playing career came to an abrupt halt, however, when he sustained a serious kidney injury. Like Fuzzy, we never saw him again.

Still, none of these memories come even close to what happened one summer day as I was hitting a tennis ball against the end of my mother's house. Up the hill from town, the longest car I'd ever seen went past me (I now know that such a vehicle is called a stretch limo). I ran into my mother's convenience store, which once served as our living room, and between gasps told her what I'd just seen going up South View. My mother looked at me as if I were stupid, so I returned to playing tennis against the wall outside. After a few minutes, I heard our telephone ringing. I knew it was ours, because we were the only family within seven streets that had one. Next thing, my mother came flying out of the house, grabbed me by the arm, and dragged me in the direction of Prince Street, two streets up South View. Soon we were making our way up the front path to Grace Jones' house. Grace worked as a nurse at Panteg Hospital with my mother. Grace ushered us into her dining room and there, sitting at Grace's dining table, was the handsomest man I'd ever laid eyes on. Beautiful, even white teeth were set in beautifully tanned skin. He was immaculately groomed, wearing sunglasses and a Homburg hat. I was totally flabbergasted! Who could this Prince of Men be?

Well, the man was Grace's cousin, Ray Jones. Actually, Reginald Alfred John Truscott-Jones, to give his full name, but he is perhaps better known by his acting name of Ray Milland. The Hollywood idol! In his younger days, he'd worked as a mill hand at one of our local steelworks and had accordingly taken this as his stage name. I cannot remember what conversation took place on that day, because I was absolutely star-struck for around twenty minutes. Here I was, in the same room as the man who had recently won the Oscar for Best Actor in the film *Lost Weekend* (1946) and who would later star with Grace Kelly in the Alfred Hitchcock thriller *Dial M For Murder*. This man was a legend in his own lifetime, and I was breathing in the same air that he was breathing out!

By the time I came back to earth, the whole incident was over, but that day I'd learned something that would stay with me for the rest of my life: If you want to be famous, then go where fame is. If you want to be successful, go wheresuccess is. Don't stay at home waiting for fame and success to seek you out, because that will rarely ever happen. My awakening was this: to reach any level of notoriety or fame, I would have to go out and seek it. This is the one premise that has driven me throughout my life to travel far in search of new horizons and new adventures.

Two
The Move

By the summer of my sixteenth year, I had graduated from Abersychan Technical College with seven General Certificates of Education. This was mainly due to the diligence of the teachers who taught me that learning was fun. They also took us on two field trips: one to a coal mine and the other to a steelworks. The main thing I came away with on both occasions was how proud these companies were of how few people had been killed while working for them during the previous year.

As far as I was concerned, if even one person died while being employed, it was one too many. This was a major wakeup call so far as employment options were concerned, and my rate of learning greatly increased after these two eye-opening visits.

My friend Russell Ivory finally persuaded me to take the entrance examination for the apprentice program at Girling Ltd. (Cwmbran). Unbeknownst to me, he had also persuaded two of my other good friends, John Harris and Trevor Roberts, to do the same.

I should explain that our school had just come off two successful years as our rugby team was very good. I first represented the school at fifteen, but the second--and last--year, was an exceptional year. If I remember correctly, we were undefeated. This little- known fact had not escaped the attention of Russell Ivory's father, who was the apprentice supervisor for Girling Ltd.

Only sixteen new trainees were accepted by Girling Ltd. that year out of 240 applicants, and four of them were from the very same Abersychan Technical College victorious team. Two other boys from that team, Bobby Malson and Cliffie Pearce, decided to go their separate ways, but what absolutely superb players they were. Ray Watkins, another player of note, went on to play for my beloved Pontypool team as did John Harris a few years later. John, incidentally, had been capped for Wales School Boys at both the under-15 and under-16 levels and was a player of enormous talent.

After the summer school break, I reported for work at the apprentice school, and after a two-hour introduction, the other new inductees were dismissed, except for the four previously mentioned Abersychan Tech boys. We were ushered into a side room and were confronted by the captain of the apprentice rugby team. Graham Bevan was his name, and he would attain fame three years later when he succeeded the famous Bryn Meredith in the middle of Newport R.U.F.C.'s front row.

He told us straight away that we had been automatically selected to play the first game of the season in two days' time. He questioned each of us about the positions that we preferred to play, then, after instructing us to be at the King's Head pub in Pontnewydd at 6:00 p.m. on Wednesday evening, he left the room. That was to be our first game in the Newport Junior Rugby Union. That particular game ended when the referee abandoned the game after a huge melee broke out. We were winning at that point, and so the victory was, technically, ours.

Our final game that season was, surprisingly enough, against the very same team in the Cup Final at Newport's famous Rodney Parade, where we once again ran out winners by three tries to two field goals (nine points to six). However when we were on the public bus going down from Ponty-pool to Newport, a strange thing happened: the bus stopped at Pontnewydd, and who should get on but John Hyatt, an ex-Abersychan Tech player, two years our senior. He was now playing for our rivals and came to the back of the bus where we were sitting, and in a condescending tone announced that since we were also Abersychan Tech boys, we were invited by him to his team's victory party after the game. He even went so far as to tell us that his team had already ordered all the food and beer.

We didn't say too much, but inwardly we were furi-ous. Before we left the locker room to play this game, Graham Bevan gave a rousing pre-game speech. At the end of this, he asked if anyone had anything else to say. John Harris related the story of John Hyatt's invitation; if there was any one thing that could have been said to galvanize our team, that was it.

We played like men possessed. After we had won that day, we found neither hide nor hair of any of our demoral-ized opponents. I was especially pleased because I had scored a touchdown with minutes to go, which sent the game into overtime, as our opponents at that point were leading three to nothing. That night, after many celebratory drinks, I slept past Pontypool and was awakened as the bus was being driven through the Pontnewynydd bus wash at the depot two miles farther up the valley.

The next day I took out my trophy to show my moth-er, only to find that it had been bent. This had probably hap-pened during the raucous party that we had experienced the previous night, but that party was entirely ours.

I played for that talented team for another two years and had the pleasure of playing alongside Eric "Goopie" Phil-lips and Paul Watts, to name but two. At the start of the 1959-60 season, Mr. Ivory called me into his office and, out of the blue, asked me how I felt about moving to work at a new

8

factory that Girling Ltd. was about to open in Cheshire (England). This was a complete shock to me, and my first thoughts were about local girlfriends, rugby, and the upheaval this would cause me. I thanked him, but said no.

When I arrived home that evening, I ran up the stairs to my bedroom and pulled out my atlas. I turned to the county of Cheshire and looked for Bromborough. After a while, there it was. My God, it was just across the River Mersey from Liverpool where there was currently an explosion of music that was driving everyone wild — —the Mersey Beat.

After much soul searching, the next morning found me knocking on Mr. Ivory's door at 8:00 a.m. I told him that

I had changed my mind, and if the offer was still on the table, I would accept. He then told me to pack my bags, because the following Monday I would be on a train heading north to Merseyside.

Before moving on, at this point, I would also like to thank the late Jack West and his family for the help and guidance that was given to me when, as a raw, fatherless and naive boy from the Eastern Valley, I needed it most. I would also like to mention all the thugs and hooligans from Blaenavon to Newport, whose continual harassment also played a part in this historic decision of mine to leave the Welsh valleys forever.

Three
The Reward

Once again the number four came up, because, like the previous move from the Tech to Girling's, I was not alone on my trek north. The apprentice school was divided into two. One part of the school concentrated on the Tool and Die program, while the other part specialized in the Machine Tool set-up program. Because the Merseyside was highly unionized, no machine set-up men could be employed from outside of that area. We were, however, technically only machine set-up apprentices, and that was the loophole that Girling Ltd. used to fox the local unions.

In 1959 there were four of us with three years' experience under our belts, and we were the four selected to take on the setting up of all the new production lines for mass-producing disc brakes. Apart from myself, the four musketeers included Terry Smith, Mansell Jones, and the soon-to-be-infamous Derek "Charlie" Stephens. We were to perform the impossible. We had to start up and then keep production going on a continual basis, which we did to the total surprise and disbelief of everyone, including ourselves.

Looking back, I realize that this experience put us in good standing at the age of twenty-one on finishing our apprenticeship. We were each promoted into positions which were, at the very least, five years in advance of anything we would have been offered had we let our lives run their normal course. What Ray Milland had unwittingly taught me was already paying dividends.

We all stayed at Ma Buckley's guesthouse in Rock Ferry, a suburb of Birkenhead, found for us by the Girling Ltd. personnel department. Once I got settled in at work,

I began looking for a new rugby club, and, because I didn't have a car, it had to be one near at hand. I found out from the locals that the nearest rugby club was Port Sunlight that played at a sports complex called the Oval on Old Chester Road. If you ever saw the film *Chariots of Fire*, it was the Oval that was used to depict the stadium where the Paris Olympic Games took place. So it was a pretty impressive setup, much grander than anything I had previously experienced. The whole setup was financed by Lever Brothers, now known as Unilever, the soap manufacturers, who had very deep pockets.

I started off playing for their Third XV but quite quickly moved up through the Second XV and then into the First XV, which at that time had several Cheshire representatives in the side. We played all the local big clubs — — New Brighton, Liverpool, Waterloo, Birkenhead Park, Manchester, and quite a number of the local Old Boys sides — — Wirralians, Parkonians, Birkonians, Instonians, Rockferians, and so on. We also ventured out farther to places like Chester, Widnes, Wrexham, Southport, and we also played in the Cheshire and National Cups. All in all I was enjoying myself, traveling farther to games than when in Wales and playing some excellent rugby.

At the end of my first season in English rugby, Lever Brothers held a sports banquet for all their teams. Rugby, football, hockey, tennis, etc., all came together at Hume Hall (named after Lord Leverhume) in Port-Sunlight Village, and we all had a wing-ding of a time. After the main dinner and speeches, we adjourned to the bar at which time the evening's entertainment, a band, started the music.

I was at the bar drinking with Dennie Bonner, Bobby Lewis, and Tony Griffiths, when I suddenly realized how good the entertaining band was. I asked someone to pass me a program so I could find out who the band was, and there it was: music provided by the Beatles. Now at this stage, they hadn't reached the fame and dizzying heights that were ahead of them but damn they were good. This was the type of music that I had come north to find out more about, and here it was.

During the intermission, I needed to visit the restroom, and on my way there, I passed the "Five Scousers" who were in the anteroom taking a break. I told them I thought their music was fabulous, and they all seemed to appreciate that. They all smiled and thanked me, almost in unison. Of course, there was no Ringo, just John, Paul, George, Pete Best, and Stuart Sutcliffe. Go to famous places if you want to meet famous people.

The next time I saw them was at the New Brighton Tower Ballroom, where I was attending the Liverpool University Rag Ball. I was with Terry, Mansell, Charlie, and I have a sneaky feeling that my buddy Pete Morrell was with us. Pete had come up the year after our initial trek north as had Lennie Caddick and "Tex" Sullivan. That night was a blast. The Beatles were the headliners, supported by Rory Storm and the Hurricanes, Freddie and the Dreamers, Gerry and the Pacemakers, and a stream of lesser-known bands that played on endlessly.

Funny enough, Gerry and his boys were playing at a small Territorial Army Hall just off Queens Drive in Liverpool the night that I met my first wife-to-be. She was a Liverpool girl from Knotty Ash, which is Ken Dodd country. Pete Morrell and I, having played rugby, decided to see what all the noise was about and stumbled into the hall.

It was so easy to see groups back then. Almost every bar had live music, and the whole Merseyside area was arocking and a-jumping.

Moving forward almost three years, my friend Lennie Caddick and I were doing a pub-crawl in downtown Liverpool.

It was just before shut tap, and we were in a bar called The Crocodile discussing what our next move should be. The clubs back then opened at 11:00 p.m., and I said to Lennie that if we left right then, we would beat the rush and stand a chance — — as nonmembers — — of getting into one.

We downed our drinks, and I headed over to Seal Street with Lennie close in tow, straight to the Pink Parrot. (I have lately gone back, but it is now a derelict house.) We bribed the bouncer at the door, and he told us that the bar was downstairs, below ground level. We stumbled down in the semi-darkness, and as we entered the bar, I could see by the dimmed lights around the bar, the silhouette of the barmaid leaning on the bar in conversation with two equally silhouetted men. She looked at us as we approached the bar, and I inquired of her if the bar was open yet, to which she said that it was.

I ordered a drink each for Lennie and myself, and then thinking my interruption might have been considered rude, I offered the two other men a drink also. We all got our drinks and were now in conversation with the barmaid and her two friends. When my eyes adjusted to the dim light, I realized that Lennie and I were drinking with John Lennon and Paul McCartney. We tried to act as normal and as casual as possible, not to blow — — probably — — the one and only chance we would ever get to meet them because by this time they were mega-famous and had recently invaded America.

After about fifteen minutes, some other people began filing in, and John and Paul had to make an abrupt exit for the emergency door. Before leaving, they turned and asked if we would like an autograph, as I genuinely felt they enjoyed our company. Lennie said that he would, but I could see they were becoming a little nervous as other people were beginning to look in our direction. I shook their hands and thanked them saying that just meeting them was enough for me. They smiled and left hurriedly.

You can imagine how many times since that magical September of 1964 I've regretted my moment of chivalry. I am told that Lennie lives in Alberta (Canada), and if I know him, he has those babies up on his wall. I, on the other hand, have since bought a framed black-and-white photograph of the Fab Four with reproduction autographs on it. I can never get George's now for, like John, he has passed on. I can only hope that one day I might meet Paul again and finally get that autograph.

I read somewhere that the Clarke family motto is Carpe Diem (Seize the Day). Why didn't I know that back then?

Four
The Conversion

The seventeen years I spent on Merseyside were really exciting. On the rugby side, I left Port Sunlight and joined a little known team called Lucas Merseyside (Joseph Lucas being the parent company of Girling Ltd.). This took me into a completely different rugby environment.

These young men were apprentices and ex-apprentices of the two Liverpool-based Lucas companies and were salt-of-the-earth, blue-collar workers. I became very good friends with John O'Donnell, Johnie Malloy, Vinnie Stockdale, Dougie Hamer, and many others.

The interesting rugby aspect was their schedule included top-heavy Lancashire rugby league styled teams. We played Widnes, Warrington, St. Helens, Wigan, Leigh, Prescott, Helsby, Orrell, Ormskirk, and, of course throughout the Liverpool area such as Sefton, Halewood, Garston, Chilwall, etc. These were indeed tough, tough teams. Although these teams were rugby union, you could see the rugby league influence the minute they came onto the park. They passed the ball off their chests in a less fluent, but equally effective, movement.

In these cities, the high schools all had rugby league

teams, and I am inclined to think that league is a tougher game all round than union. Because of the straight-ahead approach, they are much more inclined to bulldoze their way through. They also gang tackle with two, three, and even four men, and when you make a breakaway, both the wings cover back at great speed. If you were attacking them and attained an overlap on the outside, their wing man would not be drawn into a tackle, even at the expense of backing up, and this gave his support players time to come across. As soon as he felt that the inside man was covered, only then would he commit to the outside player.

I can remember relating this style of play to my friends in the Valley when I returned home to Wales on the occasional weekend. Now in the early 1970s Wales had a fantastic national team, and I could never understand why England, with all this wealth of talent up north, confined their selection to the major London clubs and Oxford and Cambridge University with perhaps one token player from one of the less fashionable clubs.

I had said many times over that when England began selecting the more rugged and tough players from up north, the whole scenario was going to change. I hate to say "I told you so," but from the mid-1980s on, the balance of power began to shift, and now England is one of, if not the, best teams in the world. Although in 2005, Wales won the Grand Slam for the first time since 1978.

Unlike us gentlemen in the union game, these guys took everything personally. When I injured an opposing player in a game at St. Helens, he went to the hospital, got fixed up, and was soon back, standing on the touchline in his street clothes. With his sleeves rolled up, he had returned to settle the score after what he had conceived was a late tackle. Even in the clubhouse afterward, he would not accept the apology— —in the form of a beer— —and vowed the next time we met, I would be the one going to hospital.

In another game at Winnington Park, I latched on to

the opposing half-back's signals. The scrum-half went blind. I knew his outside half's call, gave it, and ran between them to intercept and score under the post. In the clubhouse after the game, they were at the bar arguing about how their system had gone wrong. When I told them what I had done that day, I received very similar veiled threats about how I would never conceive children again after our next encounter.

On another occasion I was haring down the middle of the field straight toward the opponents' posts. On hearing the sound of the two wingers closing in on me ten yards from the line, I ducked to the ground leaving them on an unstoppable collision course. They collided with great impact and were strewn all over the ground, at which point I got up and strolled over under the post. From that day on, I was known at Waterloo as "that cheeky little Welsh bugger," a name which I accepted with much relish.

I took the Lucas Merseyside rugby team down to the Lucas seven-a-side tournament at Birmingham and ended up winning the final against my old Girling Cwmbran team. We won six points to three, and I happened to score the try (touchdown) and field goal to give us the victory. The following year we should have repeated, but in the semi-final, a certain winger, who shall remain nameless, held onto the ball instead of passing as I screamed past him at an unstoppable rate of speed. A simple pass was all that was needed to win the game. Instead, for some inexplicable reason, he denied us victory. Instead of winning by three points, we lost by two, giving our opponents the chance to play a substandard team in the final and certain victory, which they did by some thirty points.

I returned to Port Sunlight after two years and again had to start in the Third XV and work my way back up to the first team. This time it was not as easy as they had picked, in my absence, three very good backs in Alan Kinshott, Roger Dunhill, and Chris Lowther. It was a four-way dogfight, which actually made for an extremely competitive situation.

After several more years, I was coaxed away to play for Old Rockferians over at Prenton Park, Birkenhead, but after one season, I was back at Port Sunlight. The main reason for that was that at Old Rocks their ground did not drain too well. This meant that for most of the season it was extremely soft on top. Since I was a lightweight, this tended to slow me down a little and not allow me to perform at my best. I will, however, always remember Old Rocks as being the last team that I played seven-a-side rugby for.

We played at the Shell Sevens tournament at Ellesmere Port, and after five tough games, in which I scored a try in each, we reached the final against Wallasey (of Flock-of-Seagulls fame). At the end of two ten-minute halves, there was no score. After a two-minute break, we played an additional ten minutes overtime. Still no score. In the ninth minute of the second period of extra time--that's thirty-nine minutes in all--the Wallasey scrum-half literally crawled on his hands and knees over the line.

At that particular moment, all of the other players from both teams were collapsed on the ground. Everyone at the tournament went nuts. It was hailed as the best final ever to have been seen at this tournament, and at the party afterward, I quite honestly was so exhausted that I sat in one corner of the clubhouse and never moved all night.

The last game I played for the Lucas team was at Lymm (home of Bobby Charlton) just south of Manchester. This game was of note to me because I scored a try, directly from the kickoff, dummying through the opposition in just twenty seconds! Those King Street practice games did show some benefits.

Five
The Running

My other great sports love was athletics. While in Wales, I was part of a very successful Girling's team. In the winter, at the same time that I was playing rugby, we would run a five-mile cross-country race on Saturday morning and then play a game of rugby in the afternoon.

Pat Wallace, the international cross-country runner, was our coach, and the team consisted of Mansell Jones, Pete Morrell, George Edmunds, Seth Williams, Tony Basset, David Aston, and myself. We had some fabulous team results, but probably the best was at Gilwern where we finished third at the Welsh Nationals, coming close behind the two powerhouse Cardiff clubs: Roath and Birchgrove Harriers. In the summer, we switched to track events, and this had a special attraction for me, because prizes were awarded for the first three places in each event. Our team had some exceptional athletes: Duncan Carter, Michael "Nat" Cole, George Stinchcombe, and "Nipper" Hollister, to mention but a few. We would clean up like bandits.

I was only being paid around three pounds (twelve dollars at that time) per week, so to supplement my earnings, I would often sell my prizes to some of the management staff

19

for cold cash. One of my best customers was Jock Blackstock, the company's personnel manager. I sold him a shooting stick/seat for three pounds-which doubled my weekly earnings for that week.

One summer night, on returning from the all-company Lucas sports meeting at Birmingham, the team bus dropped me off at the bottom of George Street by Woolworth's in Pontypool. I was walking up the hill to my mother's house when, out of the darkened doorway, I heard the dreaded, "What's all this then?"

From the doorway stepped Police Constable Window. I must admit that at 2:00 in the morning, someone carrying a large duffel bag bulging with goods would clearly seem somewhat suspicious.

He asked me what I was carrying, and when he opened the bag, his eyes opened widely. He asked me to accompany him to the police station because my explanation— —that I had won all these goods at an athletic meeting— —seemed a little far-fetched to him. We arrived at the station where all the items were taken from the bag and displayed on a long table: rosewood china, crystal glassware, binoculars, watches, etc. All brand new and still in the original packaging— —as if taken straight from a retail store.

I was asked if anyone could corroborate my story, and the only person that I could think of who owned a telephone was Mr. Ivory (the apprentice supervisor) who lived at Llantarnam. I heard the sergeant put the call through, and most of the conversation was him repeating, "Really?"

He put the phone down and reentered the room where I was sitting and said to a young policeman, "Get this boy a cup of tea."

By this time everyone on duty at the station that night was sitting around the table of goods, and when during the conversation I happened to mention that I sometimes sold off my prizes, an auction broke out. I left the station wishing them good night, my duffel bag considerably lighter, and my pocket considerably bulging with cash. The only item that I refused to sell was the rosewood china tea set. That was for my mother, and she loved it.

Since moving north, I had resumed my interest in athletics. A group of us, all rugby players, began training on the track at Port Sunlight Oval to keep fit through the summer. The backbone of the team was Norman Astles, Brian Adams, Steve Hunt, and I. Apart from us serious track-runners, we had a good bunch of other (less serious) team members who entered every other type of novelty race. We all trained hard, and, come the day of the Girling Ltd. Cwmbran company sports, we all loaded onto a bus and made the 150-mile journey south.

By the end of that Saturday, after putting in a tremendous effort throughout the day, all points were tallied, and Girling Ltd. Bromborough (Cheshire) had swept the board. It was an absolutely wonderful achievement, and once again I had faced my previous teammates and come off victorious.

I must give a special mention to the ladies of that team who upheld their half of the event with great tenacity. I believe their captain was Lorraine Boynton.

I did not continue my love of cross-country running, because the terrain on the Wirral was completely different, extremely flat and very citified, compared to Cwmbran, which was hilly and more rural. While at Cwmbran, I was part of the team that went to the All-Lucas Company cross-country relay race and won it for three consecutive years. This event was held in Liverpool, and the race was run in laps around Sefton Park. For two of these three years, I also won the fastest lap around, and the third year I was beaten into second place by my teammate, from Newport (Wales), George Edmunds.

Although I had now finished my apprenticeship and was working as a methods engineer, I offered to help train the Bromborough apprentices to prepare for that same event. They were a good, hard-working bunch of boys. Many of their names escape me, but I do recall Del Haines and Colin

Heald.

As a warm-up, I entered them in a similar event at the Wallasey Sports Festival (at New Brighton), and they came in a commendable third. On paper, their times were looking-pretty good as, having been a runner of that race, I knew exactly what had to be achieved. I used an old Pat Wallace trick, on the day of the race, and led off with my slowest runner. Pat's theory was that every other team would put their fastest or second fastest runner on the first leg, and this would draw our slow runner into achieving his best result. This backfired as our slowest runner came in two minutes slower than his best time over that distance, and I knew right there that something was very wrong. My next three runners, however, all improved their best times and closed the gap on the winners to finish a good second position. The honors that day went to Cwmbran and their coach, my old buddy Pete Morrell.

That evening, at the end-of-race gathering, the story leaked out that our first leg runner had been seen the previous night out drinking around the bars in Liverpool. Had I known this, I would have taken him out of the race and put in my reserve runner whose time for the same distance, on the day, would have given us the win.

As the saying goes, "It's all part of life's rich pattern." Win or lose, these events were ideal situations for putting the metal of young men to the test.

Six
The Connection

My pal Pete Morrell and I always kept in touch even after he had decided to return to South Wales. At the end of our apprenticeship, we were all given the option to stay at Bromborough (Cheshire) or return to Cwmbran (Monmouthshire). Terry Smith, Derek Stevens, and I decided to stay, but others like Pete, Mansell Jones, and later Geoff West, for varying reasons, decided to return to their families and South Wales. Both Peter and I played rugby, but we also liked to play football.

At Port Sunlight RUFC, for instance, our Tuesday night training session consisted of playing football, which got the aches and pains out after Saturday's rugby match. For this training, we joined the Port Sunlight Soccer Club, whose coach was a famous professional ex-player named Dave Hickson. This man in his time had played for Aston Villa in Birmingham and Liverpool F.C.'s cross-town rivals, Everton F.C. To play with this man was a delight because, though in his early forties, he was still an excellent player/coach. His coaching was to put me in good shape many years later when I emigrated to America and began playing football as my number-one sport. I would continue to visit Wales, and Pete would continue to visit Merseyside. On one of Pete's visits, we decided that, for a change, we would go to Chester for a night out. Chester has to be one of my all-time favorite cities. It is an old Roman fortress town and, like Caerleon (in Gwent), is steeped in history. This particular night, we were doing our standard pub-crawl when we stumbled into "The Dublin Packet" near the marketplace. We were in conversation with the barman concerning all the old black-and-white photos and football memorabilia displayed around the walls.

He pointed to the owner, who was sitting on a high stool in one corner, and said, "That's Dixie Dean." Now, and just for the uninitiated, Dixie Dean was, and perhaps still is, the holder of the most goals scored in a single season in any division of the English Football League. I believe the number was fifty-four, or thereabouts, which is an incredible record for all times. We waved to him to come and join us, and, to our shock and amazement, when he stood up he only had one leg. Apparently diabetes had taken his leg, but not, as he put it to us, his shooting leg. What an honor it was for us to be in the company of someone who in his time had been the best at what he did. I remember thinking at that time that this was an event that I would probably never be able to repeat. I did, however, attain dizzy heights in later times at another famous meeting, and I will tell you about that later.

Another extremely enjoyable event occurred with Pete Morrell a few years later. He had come up to Merseyside for the weekend, and I had miraculously obtained tickets to see Liverpool play Coventry at Anfield Park. I was working in Liverpool at the time, and my office on Green Lane was opposite the city bus depot. It was also next door to a pub called the Wellington. For obvious reasons, this was known locally as the Boot.

The owner of this pub, Norman Ackers — — or "Knackers" to his mates — — had gotten me the tickets and told me to be at his pub with Pete at about 1:00 p.m. The game kicked off at 2:30 p.m. We were having a few pre-game drinks, and I kept looking at my watch and protesting that we should be leaving so as not to miss the kickoff. Knackers assured us that all was well and not to worry — — and, by the way, have another drink. At 2:10 p.m. we were the only three people left in the bar, except for a little old geezer named Ernie, who up until then I hadn't noticed because he had his head buried in a newspaper.

At a signal from Knackers, Ernie left the bar, and about two minutes later a large green double-decker bus pulled up in front of the Boot with Ernie behind the wheel. Ernie had borrowed our ride from the bus depot across the street and by using the bus-only lanes, got us to Anfield in record time.

As we climbed the stairs to our stand seats and sat down, the game immediately kicked off. Perfect timing! The only damper to that day was that Coventry won one to nothing. Their tall, blonde left-winger from Scotland, named Tommy Hutchinson, scored the winner. It didn't dampen our spirits too much, because that evening we celebrated our loss at the Wookey Hollow.

In the same vein, I visited Pontypool at one time, and Mansell Jones and I, on a similar pub-crawl, found ourselves in a little pub in New Inn. The pub was called the Lower New Inn, and again I made a comment about all the Manchester United photos and souvenirs festooning the walls. The man serving us said they were all his, from his playing days with Manchester United. This man, now the owner of the pub, was one of the few survivors of the 1957 Munich air disaster when almost all of that wonderful team had been wiped out when their plane crashed. His name was Colin Webster, and he, like Bobby Charlton, had been one of only six people to survive that horrible event.

Colin was originally from the Swansea area and went from there to Manchester, but after the plane crash, he was never the same player. If I remember correctly, he was a center-forward-cum-inside-forward and after finally being released by Manchester United, he went to Cardiff City and ended his playing career at Newport County. I remember seeing on TV Bobby Charlton collapse in uncontrollable tears when United eventually won the European Cup (1968). He was, no doubt, remembering all those talented young men who died while attempting that very goal. They were known as the Busby Babes, after their coach Matt Busby (later to become Sir Matt).

On another occasion, I met Jimmy "Jinkie" Johnstone, the Celtics player, who won the European Cup in 1967. It was in Harry Hood's pub at Bellshill, just outside Glasgow. He had his mother and a friend with him, and I was with my regional manager at Goliath, John Laughlin.

Whenever I visited my Goliath office at Washington, Co., Durham, I used to go for lunch at a centrally located canteen in an industrial park. Sunderland F.C. had their training ground just across from my office. It was quite common for me to walk in there and sit a few tables away from the whole team, the famous team that won the 1973 F.A. Cup, by beating Leeds United one to nothing under he management of Bob Stokoe. I don't remember them all, but Jim Montgomery, the goalkeeper, and Bobbie Kerr stand out.

I met Billy Bonds and Frank Lampart (senior) in the elevator of a Leeds hotel. They were playing for West Ham United (the "Hammers") against Leeds the next day in an F.A. Cup round. At another time, Bobby Moncur, the ex-Newcastle United captain, against Liverpool in another F.A. Cup final, picked me up in his taxi one night. We had a nice chat about soccer during the fifteen-minute run back to my hotel, but I didn't mention his three to nothing drubbing at Wembley.

On a different occasion, I was sitting in an exclusive Buxton (Derbyshire) hotel lobby when a page passed me paging Mr. Bobby Moore. Obviously, my interest was piqued. When this England captain made himself known, the page brought him to a table not more than twelve feet from where I was sitting. He was joined by a jewelry salesman, who began to show him samples out of a briefcase. This was extremely interesting, because it was about six months after the 1970

Mexico World Cup, where a jewelry shop assistant had accused Bobby of stealing from his store. The whole affair had finally been swept under the carpet, and Bobby was exonerated, but it sure sent some red flags up in my mind.

Lastly, I would like to mention a wonderfully polite and gentlemanly associate who I worked with at Girling Ltd. (Bromborough)— —Peter Farrell, the Everton and Ireland football player.

Seven
The Celebrity

In Pontypool (Wales) at the top of the Barley (Twm Barlwm) was a farm run by the Evans family. Actually it was a small holding, because the mountain was too unforgiving to allow crops to grow. The Evans family had some sheep, cows, pigs, chickens, and an endless number of dogs.

There were only two ways up to the farm by vehicle. One way was from the Tranch end, near the Sally public house. The other was from the Cwmfrwdwr end, near the Plas-y-Coed public house. I know these lanes well, because when I was involved with athletics, I ran them every weekend.

Apart from the Evans, the only other people living on the top of the Barley were the Stephens. Brian Stephens and his family lived right next to the Evans, and even higher up were Glynis and Doreen Stephens and their families. I believe the two families were related, and to get to their houses by vehicle you had to go up to Pant-y-Gasseg and come back down over the mountaintop.

In the spring and summer, it was beautiful up there, and I spent many a happy hour roaming all over the hills. In the winter, it was bleak and desolate— —a tough and uncompromising place to live!

My older sister, Bunny (Patricia Ann, actually), did her nursing training at Cardiff Royal Infirmary. She was transferred to Pontypool General Hospital where she worked in the emergency department (called Casualty or A&E in the UK).

One day a man brought his young son into the ER for treatment to a nasty gash on his leg. Naturally my sister tended to the boy and asked his father how the injury had happened. The man explained that he had recently bought Evans' farm. His son had climbed up onto one of the out buildings, and his foot had broken through the rusty, old corrugated tin roof. He'd then become firmly entrapped. They'd had a devil of a time freeing him because he'd been stuck fast up to his thigh.

After seeing to the boy's leg and having given him a painful anti-tetanus shot, my sister had time to take a good look at the man. She told him that, although she could tell from his accent that he wasn't a Pontypool man, she had the feeling that she'd seen him before. The man then identified himself, and it turned out that he was the actor Ronald Lacey. He'd bought the Evans' farm to use as a retreat between acting jobs. He asked my sister to keep this to herself, as he really needed peace and quiet whenever he came to Pontypool.

Apart from our family, Bunny never told a soul, and this was much appreciated by Mr. Lacey. Whenever she happened to bump into him while shopping in Pontypool, he would talk to her as if they'd been friends for years. I have a photograph, which I treasure to this day, of Ronald Lacey, my mother, my sister, and my cousin. It's sad to think that everyone in that photo has now passed on.

One of Mr. Lacey's last movies was *Raiders of the Lost Ark* in which he played the evil Nazi interrogator who burned his hand when picking up the holy medallion. I mention all this now because very few people in Pontypool ever knew that the famous actor was walking around in their midst——a fact probably attributable to my sister's vow of silence and the promise she made to him. Naturally, I have his autograph, and instead of signing it Ronald Lacey, he signed it "Heil, Hitler, from Toht" — — the character he so ably played in the never-to-be-forgotten Raiders mega-hit!

One weekend, I came home to Pontypool from Cheshire for a visit, and it happened to coincide with the British Marathon trials for the up-coming Olympic Games. This event was based at Cwmbran Stadium (which didn't exist during my running days).

The runners began with a lap of the stadium and then took off out onto the roads for a run that would take them around the country roads and then back to the stadium for a last lap before the finish line. It was a major event for our area My good buddy Pete Morrell and I were envious that, after all the miles of running we'd done on those very roads, we could not get into the stadium, because of the tight security. We actually drove the roads in my car and watched the progress of the race firsthand.

We were coming up the hill by the Upper Cock pub in Croesycelliog when we came across a runner that was clearly experiencing some difficulties. He was weaving all over the road, and it was clear to Pete and me that this guy was not going to make it. I drew up alongside him and asked if he needed assistance, at which point he collapsed over the hood of my car.

I winked at Pete and said, "I think we've got our ticket into the stadium!"

We loaded the guy into the car, and in no time at all, we were being ushered into the stadium where we took the runner straight to the first aid station. The guy was very grateful and so were we, as the stadium was ours for the rest of the day! We sat in the stands, watched the whole event in its entirety, and had an extremely nice but illicit afternoon.

On another occasion Pete, using the Clarke method of "never let them stop you," was able to gate-crash John Toshack's benefit dinner at a hotel in Liverpool. Whensomeone approached his table with a questioning look, Pete explained that he knew "Tosh" from his Swansea days, at which the man sent a round of drinks over to "Tosh's Welsh friends."

Someone once told me that the only limitations you experience in life are those which you place on yourself. With this in mind and a confident approach, almost all things are possible, and almost any door can be opened. It is a question of if you want something badly enough, there is usually a way of getting it (if you apply your mind to it).

Eight
The Career

It might surprise a lot of people that, while all these extracurricular activities were going on, I actually did have a career as well.

A five-year engineering apprenticeship, three at Cwmbran and two at Bromborough, was followed by three years as a methods engineer at Girling Ltd. on Merseyside. After eight years with the same company, I began to realize that it was time for me to move on. I also realized that working inside factories was not the life for me.

As a methods engineer, I worked very closely with a number of our suppliers' field representatives, and it seemed to me that their lifestyle of traveling from factory to factory was more in keeping with what I wanted to do. Not only would this give me the freedom to move about relatively unsupervised, but it also afforded me a car provided by the company plus an expense account.

One of Girling Ltd.'s main suppliers was a company called Sandvik, a Swedish company, and I asked their sales rep, Bill Owen, how I should proceed. He told me that his company would be expanding and employing more salesmen in about a year. He said he'd recommend me for such a position when that time came. He also advised me that, if in the meantime I could get another company to take me on as a salesman, this experience would further strengthen my position.

I studied the Liverpool Echo newspaper for several weeks and then finally spotted just what I was looking for. A company in Coventry named B.O. Morris Ltd. was looking for a new salesman for a position on Merseyside, and I knew their product range. I applied for this position and after two interview visits to their company headquarters was offered the job, which I gladly accepted.

The sales territory that I was given included all the automotive manufacturers in Merseyside, plus all their Tier-I and Tier-II suppliers such as Girling Ltd., the company I had worked for. This gave me the opportunity to travel all over Liverpool, Birkenhead, Chester, Ellesmere Port, Runcorn, Widnes, and Warrington— —all good manufacturing towns bristling with unlimited sales opportunities for me to exploit. I knew that this job was only going to last for one year because that would be when Sandvik, a very large and prosperous company, would begin their expansion. I had specifically told Bill Owen that I had only taken this job so that I would be better qualified to work for Sandvik.

For the next twelve months, I made some nice business trips, and, more importantly, I made some very good business contacts. When the year was up, B.O. Morris Ltd. had to cut back as business generally had taken a slump, and anyway I was ready to jump ship.

Within two weeks of being let go by B.O. Morris Ltd., I was on Sandvik's payroll, doing exactly the same type of work but for more money. I was covering the same business territory, so all the contacts I had made over the past twelve months were the same people that Sandvik needed business from. As we would say in the athletic world, I was off to a flying start. The next five years were to be some of the most exciting and stimulating times of my career. I enjoyed business trips to Hanover (Germany), Bousonville (France), and Stockholm and Sandviken in Sweden. Now I began to do exactly what I had planned to do, which was to travel far and wide, because I knew that this would bring me into contact with more of the jet-setting class of people who already had the time and the money to indulge themselves in the lifestyle I yearned for.

Sandvik had the UK divided up into major sales regions, and my area of Merseyside was under the West Midlands area, managed by a gentleman called Dick Crowe. He was a tall, distinguished-looking man who was highly nervous and easily excitable. Some of the other West Midland team were Derek and Alan Gould, Tom Williams, Peter Stocking, Ken Williams, and Peter Richardson, all extremely capable engineers/salesmen. This was a fast-paced company, and I acquired an incredible amount of knowledge in the presence of this group of men.

We also had an enormous amount of fun, and our unofficial motto was "Work Hard——Play Hard," a role that epitomized my lifestyle. After five very good years, things began to stagnate somewhat, because other people in the company were envious of West Midland's sales success and thought that we were having just a little too much fun. All sorts of restraints were now put on our travel and expenses, and it became increasingly obvious that the new regime was determined to bring us to heel, and I decided— —right or wrong——that it was time to move on again.

I was now not only looking for a change of company, but also a step up into sales management. I found the opportunity with a Merseyside distribution company that belonged to a very well-known and nationally famous steel manufacturer. I am deliberately not mentioning this company's name because, although I became their regional sales manager for the next two years, it was not an enjoyable experience. Unlike Sandvik, a young, dynamic company on the cutting edge of new technology, this company was the exact opposite.

Memoirs of a Welshman

The fact that the son of my boss worked as a salesman for me didn't help either. As you can imagine, this caused me no end of problems. For two years, I had to bite the bullet and grind out a career the hard way. On more than a few occasions, I was ready to resign, but as I had set my goal to stay with them for exactly two years, I stayed. Well, guess what? Almost exactly two years later, I walked into my boss' office and handed in my resignation. He was a nice old guy who never hindered me but never exactly helped me either. His only comment was that he had been expecting this day to come a lot sooner than it had. I shook his hand, cleared my desk, and was gone.

Within two weeks, I was working for a company called Goliath Threading Tools, out of Aston, Birmingham. Now this was more to my liking. They wanted to open up a stocking depot in Liverpool to cover South Lancashire, Merseyside, the Wirral, and North Wales. I signed on as their sales manager for that reason. In no time at all, I had established a depot in Green Lane, Liverpool, and had begun calling on many of the companies that I had during my previous eight years in sales. I was young and eager, and my aggressive style of management suited them to a T.

Within eighteen months, I was made manager of their Liverpool, Manchester, Leeds, Washington (Tyne-and-Wear), Belfast, and Glasgow depots. Now I was in my element, because unlimited traveling throughout the north of England, Scotland, Ulster, and North Wales brought me into contact with a lot of famous and talented people.

Quite a number of my previous stories happened during this period. Like the time when I was in a club called Bloomers in Newcastle-upon-Tyne and met The Who——Daltry, Entwistle, Townsend, and their quirky drummer, Keith Moon. This club was on three levels, the top one being a posh lounge area, with drinks being served out of a room with one of those Dutch doors where the top could be opened, but the bottom remained shut.

I was standing there, ordering a couple of drinks when "Moonie" came up alongside. With big pop-eyes and a weird voice, he ordered a bottle of champagne in an ice bucket. I knew immediately who he was. Apparently, the next two young ladies to the bar didn't because, when he invited them to join him, they told him to "F — — — off!" As he slithered away, I turned to them and asked if they knew who they'd just turned down? When they asked, "Who?" I pointed across the room and said, "The Who," at which they almost passed out. This was around the time when the band went through their phase of smashing their guitars on stage. They also trashed quite a number of their hotel rooms, but, all in all, they were a damn fine group. I spoke to them briefly, but as more patrons began arriving, they left abruptly.

Some years later, in Detroit, Michigan, I finally went to see them play "Quadraphonia" with guests Gary Glitter and Billy Idol as heads of the Rockers and Mods. Poor old Keith Moon was a long time dead by then, under extremely suspicious circumstances.

On another visit to Newcastle, I was staying at a hotel in Washington (then County Durham). I came down in the elevator and on seeing a shoeshine machine in the lobby, I proceeded to try and use it. For some reason it would not work, so as I looked around for some assistance, I saw coming toward me two pretty, African-looking ladies. They were smiling broadly, and as they approached I asked them for assistance. I mistakenly thought that they were employees of the hotel. We all tried to fix the machine, but to no avail. It would not work. We parted company and went our separate ways.

Later that evening I entered one of Newcastle's finest nightclubs to see a performance by Sly and the Family Stone. The lights dimmed, and onto the stage came Sly's two backup singers, and guess who they were? My two housemaids from the hotel. If I had known who they were at the hotel, instead of asking for shoeshine assistance, I could have asked them to sing a few bars from one of their hit recordings. I nevermade that kind of mistaken assumption again.

Nine
The Transition

The owner and chairman of Goliath was Norman Moore, later to become Sir Norman. He was also father of the Great Britain and Olympic show-jumper, Ann Moore. She received a silver medal at the Munich games. In a jump-off for the gold medal, the Italian officer went first and recorded a good time and clear round. Ann set off on her courageous horse Psalm at a very good pace time-wise and would take the gold so long as she and her horse made a clear round. Alas, at the very last fence her horse clipped the top pole, and it rattled and, agonizingly slowly, fell to the ground.

I remember Sir Norman flew to Munich because of the capture and assassination of the Israeli athletes, but Ann was safe, as her event was being held some forty- to fifty-miles away from the athletic center where the mayhem had taken place.

After the Olympics, Ann wrote a book about her show-jumping life and which I proudly delivered to many of Goliath's good customers. I also had the privilege of meeting her and all the Moore family at their family farm in the Warwickshire countryside. I met her again at a horseracing event at Newmarket, where we were entertaining some top customers. We had a wonderful time, and one of my clients, who, unbeknownst to me, was a horse racing fan, won money on all seven races that day. A good time was had by all.

After another eighteen months, I was again promoted, this time to national sales manager, which put me in charge of all sales in England, Scotland, Wales, and Northern Ireland. This afforded me the opportunity to travel to places that I had never been before and meet many more exciting, interesting people. I was now in the position to plan my sales trips around any major sporting, music, or social event that I wished to attend. I'm not saying I did this all the time, but if something cropped up, I had no compunction in taking a detour to put me in the right place at the right time. On a business trip to Northern Ireland, I met Peter O'Docherty, in Londonderry (or "Derry," if you prefer). He was an ex-football international and, at the time of our meeting, was the buyer for one of our customers.

I also remember another Irish incident in 1974. I was walking back to my hotel in Lisburn, just outside Belfast, and was trudging up the long gravel path to the front door. The path was tree lined, and as I was crunching my way up the path, I had an eerie feeling that I was not alone. I turned around and found myself looking down the barrel of a rifle.

Standing in front of me were two British soldiers in full battle dress and camouflage. They asked me who I was, where I'd been to that night, and why I was walking alone in such a dangerous area. I answered their questions, and as a final question, they asked me to name one pub that I frequented in Liverpool. I gave them "the Rocket" up on Queens Drive to which the one, who was not asking the questions, nodded to his companion. I was then told, in no uncertain terms, to go to the hotel and not show my face again until the sun came up the next day.

With my heart beating almost out of my chest, I ran to the hotel and did not step outside again until my manager, Irvin Bothwell, came by to pick me up in the morning. It was not unusual on business trips to Northern Ireland in those days to be pulled over by the military on some lonely country road for an identity check. You always knew that while you were out of your car being interrogated, an army sniper had his crosshairs on your back.

On another occasion, I was driving down the M-6 South from Glasgow and was feeling a little drowsy. I pulled off the road at a rest stop around the Lake District, dropped my driver's seat back into the recline position, and closed my eyes to take forty winks. The next thing I was awakened by the sound of car doors slamming. Looking up, I could see that another car, a limo, had pulled up and parked right next to my car, which must have appeared unoccupied. I watched the occupants of the limo climb out and start to stretch and contort their bodies to get the kinks out.

All of a sudden, I realized who they were. It was Marc Bolan and his band T-Rex. I heard one of them pronounce in a Cockney accent, "There you are, boys! The Moors!"

I guess he could not have been very good at geography in school because the Lake District and the Moors are about a hundred miles apart. Anyway, these long-haired scalawags wandered off in the direction of the café, and I followed to see what other pearls of wisdom were to be uttered. I sat at a table for some twenty minutes or so, watching their buffoonery, and then I decided not to ask them for their autographs or to even speak to them. Unfortunately, Marc died at an early age, and the rest of the band faded into oblivion (not "Bolivia" as Mike Tyson would say!).

It was after a similar long and hard trip that I discovered I had become hypoglycemic. Many years of skipping breakfast, eating lunch on the run, and then making up for it all by eating a huge meal for dinner had thrown my sugar intake into disarray. Having too little sugar and then way too much wrecked my dietary balance to such an extent that I was now producing too much insulin— —the opposite of diabetes.

For the rest of my life I was to live with this condition; and one time, having returned to my home in Bebington, I sat down on the couch totally exhausted. When my wife called me to the dinner table, I didn't have the energy to stand up. A doctor was summoned, and he diagnosed me with the disorder.

While I'm on down events in my life, it brings to mind an episode which could have proved fatal had not the timing and the place been to my advantage.

After being punched in the face during a rugby match, the whole inside of my lower lip was gashed and quickly became ulcerated. I went to the local pharmacy and bought the strongest over-the-counter tablets, which I was assured would heal the ulcers. A side effect from these pills, however, was that I had to visit the toilet too many times. I went to the doctor and not relating the symptoms with the pills, told him of my new dilemma. He prescribed a course of other pills, which the pharmacist provided. Between them, instead of 40 grams per day when I got the pills, the dosage was 400 grams per day.

Not knowing anything was wrong with the dosage, I took the pills religiously as instructed. After a few days, I was feeling decidedly strange and light-headed. On the fourth or fifth day, I asked to be sent home from work, as I was feeling completely lifeless. Driving home from the outskirts of Liverpool, I stopped my car in the old Mersey Tunnel because I could not move my arms or legs. A traffic-jam quickly ensued, and when the police came up to my car to ask what was wrong, I told them to get me to a hospital as quickly as possible. If I was to pass out, I told them, check the pills in my jacket pocket.

I was taken by ambulance to Birkenhead General Hospital, and after checking the pills, a nurse came rushing in and gave me an injection. Within the hour, I was feeling well again. They explained to me that the pills were dehydrating me to a point where I was almost paralyzed. The pills contained Atropine, which is basically the same poison that the Amazon natives use to tip their arrows when hunting monkeys. It would paralyze the monkey, which would then fall out of the tree, thus the Indians would not need to retrieve the monkey by climbing the tree.

When I was well enough, I visited both the doctor and the pharmacist, but neither would claim responsibility, so I was left with a no-win situation. If this happened today, there would be a huge lawsuit, and if this incident had happened on some lonely stretch of highway, I would not be here to tell of it today, as my whole respiratory system would have shut down.

Ten
The Next Move

I'd worked for Goliath and Mr. Norman Moore for the better part of five years when, one day, I was summoned to his office to discuss the company and its sales in the UK. After discussing the UK sales, he proceeded to fill me in on his overview of the company worldwide. Several different countries were mentioned, and almost as a by-the-way, he told me that he was currently looking to open a stocking depot in the Detroit, Michigan, area, to service the American automotive industry. He told me that he'd been searching without success for the right candidate to fill the sales manager's position in the U.S.

I have to tell you that, ever since meeting Ray Milland as a boy of nine or ten, I had always wanted to visit the States, and this was the opportunity I'd been waiting for! In as casual a manner as possible, I mentioned that, if he continued to have trouble in this area, then I'd be only too willing to go over there and take care of this matter for him.

Several months went by, and I was again summoned to the chairman's office. Without further delay, he asked me how soon I would be able to go over to Detroit and interview some candidates who had applied to an ad currently running in the *Detroit News*.

I told him it would take about two weeks to organize some work and family-related situations, and then I'd be free to go. He suggested a one-week visit, but I suggested that a two-week visit would afford me the time required to solve this problem. I also assured him that when I returned, the problem would be taken care of.

Because of my previously successful track record, he concurred, and we agreed on a particular date, September 27, and he would arrange the air tickets and accommodations.

Playing rugby on the previous Saturday before the trip was not one of my better ideas, particularly since I told my wife that I was "just going up to the club to watch the game." I even took my son, Richard, with me to make everything kosher, but my rugby kit was still in the trunk of my car from the previous week's game. The First XV and Third XV teams were at home; the Second XV and Fourth XV had traveled away; and with ten minutes to kickoff, the III team captain came out of the dressing room and said, "Taffy, do you have your kit?"

Well, how could I refuse a last run-out? The game went well for us, and with ten minutes to go, I dived over for a try with two hard, young men hanging onto me. I scored, but the weight of the two tacklers came down on my right shoulder and dislocated it! This was the second time for this particular shoulder, and in typical fashion, I got into the car and drove myself to Clatterbridge Hospital. On reaching the car park, I flung open the driver side door, but as I was half out of the car, the door swung back, hit my shoulder, and popped it back into place! I remember thinking that, at thirty-six years of age, if my shoulder could pop in and out that easily, then it was time for me to pack up playing rugby.

Richard was sworn to secrecy about the whole incident, as back to the clubhouse we went for the post-game party. I was feeling no pain whatsoever when I got home that evening, but in the middle of the night as the alcohol wore off, I had to confess all to my wife, because I couldn't find the damn painkillers!

A few days later, I landed at Detroit Metropolitan Airport and checked into the Holiday Inn on Michigan Avenue in Dearborn. Boy, did I love America. I loved everything about it: the food, the climate, the people, the casual style of business, and, of course, the nightlife! I interviewed about a dozen applicants for the sales manager's job, and the problem became immediately apparent.

As salesmen, these people were making more money than we were offering for a manager. To cut a long story short, I had no takers. The solution was easy. Why didn't I take the job and change from UK sales manger to U.S. sales manager? This would solve the money differential and put someone into the job that would need no training. I saw my two weeks out, enjoying every day and night of it, and on the flight back, I was feeling pretty smug.

Monday of the following week I was back at Mr. Moore's office where I told him I'd solved the American problem.

When he asked me who the candidate would be (no, not The Who), I told him me. I would go to America for six months to get everything up and running, and after that, if I liked it, I'd go back for another two years. This would, of course, entail my leaving my family in Bebington. I negotiated a two-week holiday through the Christmas period, which would give me dual three-month stints in the States. The die was cast. Within a further two weeks, I was again on a plane crossing the Atlantic in a westerly direction.

I settled in remarkably smoothly having found a new and less expensive motel called the White House on Michigan Avenue, just a few miles down Telegraph Road from my office in Redford. The company, Goliath, also had an older and more established depot in Parsipany, New York, about forty miles northwest of New York City. This afforded me the opportunity to travel throughout most of New England, which-looks remarkably like old England but has better weather. There was, however, one thing that I hadn't previously experienced and which was a shock to the system — — the North American winter. Boy, when they get snow, they get about a ton of it!

Most people born and bred in the northern states have adapted to the harsh winters. They indulge themselves in skiing, tobogganing, snowmobiling, and, of all things, ice fishing (as far as I'm concerned, this is the most mundane pastime ever invented). I did, however, get hooked on ice hockey, and Detroit had the Red Wings, one of the best and most historic teams ever.

Another thing I'd never before experienced was the Midwest tornadoes. These were quite devastating to behold and also deadly. But I soon learned the difference between a tornado warning and a tornado alert. I was driving along in the Romulus area when I heard over my car radio a tornado alert for the first time. I rang my office from a pay phone, but by mistake I told my secretary there had been a tornado warning. She told me to leave my car and head for the nearest ditch!

After around thirty minutes, I phoned her back and complained that it wasn't very pleasant being in a rain-soaked ditch for all that time. At that, she laughed so hard she almost split my eardrums. I found out that the alert only meant be aware of the possible danger of a tornado and not to dive into a ditch until one was imminent!

Americans also celebrate different holidays like Labor Day and Thanksgiving. During my first three-month stint in the States, around the end of November, everyone was talking about turkey, stuffing, and all the trimmings, but I didn't pay much attention to them. The next day, a Thursday, I turned up at the office and, after letting myself in, went into my own, separate office to begin work on a lengthy report for which I needed complete concentration. About 10:00 a.m. I came out of my office, walked down the hallway, and into the main office, which I found totally still and devoid of people.

After scratching my head for half an hour, I decided to phone my secretary, Ruth Roy. I asked her where she was and what was she doing? She replied that she was stuffing a turkey. She then asked me what I was doing, and when I told her I was at the office, she split my eardrums again with that laugh of hers. Everyone had assumed that I knew Thanksgiving was a public holiday!

Eleven
The Adjustment

Across the street from the White House was a run-down bar called the Red Coach Inn, which had been an actual stagecoach stop on the Detroit-to-Chicago run. Nothing elegant, just a shot-and-a-beer bar with a pool table and a poker game that seemed to go on endlessly. I learned a lot about American pool, both eight-ball and nine-ball, at that bar. I was always good at banking balls off the rails, but I noticed that the American players, by using top and bottom on the cue ball, and left- and right-hand English also, would always position the cue ball in a good position to make their next shot real simple. I really had my work cut out against these players, and I learned very quickly, if you don't have a make-able next shot, you'd better hide the cue ball so the opponent couldn't have an easy follow-up shot, which could lead to a run-out.

My Pontypool upbringing, with the hours of practice at the snooker hall underneath the Park Cinema, stood me in good stead for these situations. Some American pool players were not too happy with these tactics, and particularly when we were playing for money, tempers would get a little frayd-wever, and if I won, I would always use the winnings to buy a drinkfor the loser, and that would usually defuse the situation.

The poker game was a similar story, with me being relatively inexperienced compared to my American counterparts. They had so many variations on the game that almost every new dealer would introduce his version of poker played by his rules. Some nights, I would sit down at the table with a West Virginian, a Michiganer, a Texan, and a Polish immigrant (who could scarcely speak a word of English). The games were long and complicated, as each player tried to adjust his game to the new rules. When it was my deal, the only thing I could think of was deuces wild or something similar.

Luckily, I met a young man, Mark Miller, whose family owned and operated one of the more famous burger bars in Dearborn. He explained all the rules to me so I wouldn't lose so much money. (He also taught me that English pontoon was the same as American blackjack, which also helped greatly.) Sometimes I would fold, no matter how good my hand was because some games were just too complicated. When the West Virginian needed to relieve tension, he would say, "I don't understand it. You northerners shit in the house and cook in the yard!" He was implying that his state was superior, because they reversed these basic chores. It would bring a momentary laugh, then there would be silence, and it was back to the game. When a certain new player from God-knows-where came into the game, however, and introduced "Deuces and Jacks, a King with the Axe, a pair of natural sevens takes it!" everyone folded.

I took my two weeks back in England for the Christmas holidays and had a nice relaxing time with family and friends. No rugby this time, as I couldn't afford a repeat of my last debacle. Soon I was back in the States, and our house in England was up for sale, because I knew that I wanted the American style of life.

By the time I got back to the States, the snow had abated somewhat, and I was able to venture out farther than the old honky-tonk across the road from the White HouseI had been told about an Irish pub, the Dublin Inn, located down in East Dearborn, where it was reputed a lot of people from the old country hung out. Work was going well, so I felt pretty good as I stepped into the Dublin.

It was like stepping back two centuries in time: thick blue cigarette smoke, the chatter of a typical old pub, and, of course, the best of Irish music accompanied by shouts and screams. I got to talking to an ex-Coventryite (I spit in Tommy Hutchinson's direction) whose mother (maiden name Faulkner) had come from a small town called Blaenavon, about five miles up the valley from Pontypool. Her name was Eileen Lemon (née Gamble), and the following week she introduced me to her husband, Bill, and their friends, Bob and Margaret Harrison.

Bob and I hit it off immediately because we were both Liverpool F.C. fans. He'd been an amazingly good football player as a schoolboy, good enough that Preston North End (one of the premier football clubs in England) had come knocking at his door. Bobby was not there at the time and his father, not realizing the significance of the situation, declined their offer without even telling Bobby what had occurred. It was quite a few years later that Bobby found out about it, and, naturally, he was "gutted." This was a double-disappointment because the whole family had, in the meantime, emigrated to Canada, so there was now no way to reverse the situation. His father's decision had been based on his thinking that his son should get a trade first.

At that time, in the Dearborn area, there was a Canadian Legion Club, which these people and many other Brits went to on a Friday night. The members were almost all British, so darts, snooker, and dominoes were the order of the night. I soon became a member, and all of a sudden I went from having no British friends in America to having a couple of hundred, overnight. This made the transition to living in America much easier as almost every weekend one or another of the CLC members had a house party.

Now, instead of searching on my own to find entertainment, I was getting invitations over the phone almost on a daily basis. What a terrific bunch of guys! They had all immigrated from Britain, some via Canada, and were almost all working as skilled craftsmen and professionals in and around the automotive industry (predominately Ford Motor Company).

These were good days. Unlike me, they were all making good money, had nice homes, big cars, and in some cases, boats. I could see that there was still good money to be made, but it appeared that the key to all this was to be working for an American company.

I returned to Britain at the end of my six-month trial period. The chairman was very pleased with the way things were going, and I was happy in my new environment. It was a match made in heaven! It was agreed: I was to return to the States on a new two-year contract, and when that was completed, the whole arrangement would be reviewed for further discussion.

I walked out of Mr. Moore's office, and if I'd been wearing a hat, I would have thrown it into the air and probably done cartwheels down the street (my shoulder permitting!). The first part of my planned move to America had been successful, and now I had a further two years to make this so-called temporary move into a permanent one.

This was going to change all of our lives, I knew — — mine, my wife's, and my children's. I had now rented a house in Dearborn, just outside of Detroit, because I was told that the school system there was one of the best in the area. Dearborn was also the home of the Ford Motor Company, which meant I was slap-bang in the middle of one of America's largest automotive manufacturers, the market to which I would be selling. The stage was set for my most daring escapades, and I was ready to perform.

Twelve
The Sting

When we arrived back in the States, there was quite a large welcoming committee to greet us, and we all quickly settled into the American way of life. My pal Bobby Harrison was coaching football in a town called Canton, and his team, The Stingers, was in the boys under-10 division. His son, Robert, was on the team, and he invited my son, Richard, to join his squad. We trained twice a week and played on the weekend, and soon I was helping out and acting as Bobby's assistant coach.

After a year, Bobby's son had to move up one age group to the under-12 division, and naturally Bobby went with him. Bobby asked me if I would coach the Stingers since my son, Richard, had another year to go in the under-10 division. Because of this, I started going to the Great Lakes Youth Soccer League meetings. This was comprised of three cities: Canton, Livonia, and Garden City. The Canton Club was run by an Englishman, Dave Monk; Livonia was headed up by a Scotsman named John Barkley; and Garden City was run by an American, Gary Prevo.

After one more year, Richard had to move up to the under-12 division, and since we lived about fifteen miles away, I came up with the idea to start the Dearborn Soccer Club and get them joined to the GLYSL. I went to the Canadian Legion Club and secured the help of three Brits (John Bricknell, Ron Dickie, and Elwyn Price) and began organizing. Basically, I took over the enrollment of children from the under-8 division to the under-18 boys. I was also able to sign up one girls' team in each of these divisions, ending up with sixteen teams to begin our first season.

I asked John Bricknell to become president as he was senior to me, plus he'd already had experience in the football arena as a referee. I did most of the running around signing up players, attending meetings with the league and the city of Dearborn, and ordering the uniforms.

Come the spring, we were ready to roll, as Dearborn became the fourth city to join the GLYSL. Outside of all this, I was also coaching two teams — —my son's team, the Hot Shots, and my daughter's team, the Hot Pants. We did well in our inaugural year with some of our teams actually winning their divisions.

The following year, I didn't have to go door-to-door as we held the registration at the Dearborn Civic Center, and, by this time, our fame had spread throughout the city. We signed up twenty travel teams and a slew of in-house teams-- around one thousand children in all. I went back again to the Royal Canadian Legion Club and persuaded other members to become soccer coaches. People like Dave Hendry, Jimmy Craig, Joe McCracken, Frank Byrne, John Bricknell, Ron Dickie, Elwyn Price, and many others too numerous to mention, who now all had teams of their own.

While all this was going on, David Monk, at the GLYSL, was preparing to step down as the league president. He and John Barkley coaxed me into becoming the new president, and although I had a great deal of work on my plate, I accepted. So, within just three years of landing in the U.S., I was president of the GLYSL, was vice president of Dearborn Soccer Club, and was also coaching two teams. I had negotiated for playing fields with four schools in Dearborn, and all of them agreed that we could use their facilities for our home matches. Stout Junior High, Smith Junior High, Bryant Junior High, and Henry Ford Elementary all gave us their blessing. The city of Dearborn Parks and Recreation asked me to meet with their director, Dick Peppard, and he told me that the city wanted to be involved in our soccer program. I told them that they could help by giving us permanent goalposts, to save having to erect and then dismantle the temporary ones, and also all four of our home fields needed to be marked out with chalk lines.

This was agreed, and then he announced they were going to appoint a soccer advisor who would be on the city's payroll. I told him that I would only allow the city to participate in our soccer program if I was given that position!

By this time, I had finished working for the English company, Goliath, my two years being up. I was now working for their best customer, Kean Manufacturing, whose owners, the Imoberstag family (the matriarch being the niece of the Henry Ford), kindly donated the soccer uniforms for all the children and even signed up some of their own children to the program. Everything was clicking along just fine!

I said that I no longer worked for Goliath. Toward the last six months of my two-year visit, I had decided that returning to Britain was not going to be an option for me. I'd heard from some of my friends back in England that the chairman wanted me to go to Australia when I returned from U.S. I didn't feel that it would be right to ask my family to make another big move, particularly since we'd all settled into our new location so well.

I was also having discussions with the head office to try to get myself a salary raise, and this was not going well. The company now intended to send out an accountant from the head office to visit us and monitor our progress. I didn't care for this idea, because it could easily be done via phone, fax, or mail, but I particularly didn't like it because the American company had to pay for the pleasure, or displeasure, of these visits.

I had already decided that I wanted to remain in the U.S. after my two-year contract was up. In the meantime, I had introduced Goliath's best customer to a British company that was manufacturing a new machine that was critical to the production of the automotive nuts produced by Kean Mfg. Their existing machines were around fifty years old. They began negotiating with the British company for the first batch of twenty new machines, but that company ran out of money before the order was completed. Kean Mfg. then had to put money into the British company to ensure the machines were made, and in return they now owned the rights and all patents to do with this product.

Kean invited me to join them as soon as my contract expired, and, as an added incentive, they would also apply for my green card. This would enable me to remain in the U.S. indefinitely. With this deal in my back pocket, I began to deliberately make a nuisance of myself in the hope that Goliath would eventually want to get rid of me.

Predictably, they took the bait and sent their accountant over to do the dirty deed of letting me go. When told that I was to be let go, I pointed out to them what would be considered some questionable accounting practices within their system. To cut a long story short, I ended up with a $12,000 severance paycheck, which shortly afterward cost the accountant his job.

The moral of this episode is "Never send a boy to do a man's job."

Thirteen
The Bonus

Around this time something amazing happened. The first National Soccer League was formed in America, and Detroit was successful in obtaining one of the franchises. The Detroit Express were to play against such teams as the New York Cosmos, the Tampa Rowdies, and the Fort Lauderdale Strikers to name a few.

To get this league off to a good start, a lot of foreign players were brought in. In fact, the teams only had to have two U.S. nationals on their roster, unlike today, which is the other way around. At Detroit, we acquired a few good British players like Sam Oates, Jim Brown, Roger Osborne, Steve Seargent, Eddie Calhoun, Mick Leach, Alan Brasil, Tony Dunne, Don Niardello, Mark Hately, Davie Bradford, Steve Earl, and last but not least, Trevor Francis. These players, unlike in Britain, were told they had to make themselves accessible to the fans at the post- game parties held at the Main Event inside the Pontiac Silverdome where the games were played. This meant that, on a social level, I mixed with all these professional players and also players from the away teams— —such players as Rodney Marsh, Ian Callaghan, Steve Heighway, David Harvey, Ted McDougall, Brian Kettle, and many more too numerous to mention.

These were exciting times. To mix one-on-one with some of the best players of their time and to be able to ask them any soccer-related questions was absolute bliss. Back home in Britain, this would have been any soccer fan's delight!

There was one other player that I spent about ten magic moments with at the bar of the Main Event. His name was George Best. If anyone would have asked me who, above all other players, was my number-one choice of people to meet at that time, he'd have been my choice. He was playing for Fort Lauderdale, and except for a slight potbelly, he still had all the touches on the ball that he had as a younger man. About fifteen minutes before the final whistle, he was substituted, and with boots in hand he trundled off down the sideline towards the dressing room.

I watched him disappear out of sight, and since I was seated at the Main Event end, as soon as the final whistle came, I was up the stairway and into the restaurant before anyone else — — or so I thought. On arriving at the bar, it became obvious that I wasn't the first as there, leaning against the bar, was Georgie. The barman was further down the bar with his back to us, and he was checking the optic measure bottles. I gave a loud "Ahem," at which he came over to the two of us and asked me what we were drinking.

"A pint for you, George?" I asked. With a nod and a gleam in his eye, we settled back for a chat. I didn't make the same mistake as with the Beatles. I asked him straight away for his autograph, which he gladly gave, and I still have and treasure it to this day.

Ian Callaghan then came over to George and told him their coach was leaving, so we shook hands, and he was on his way. I did manage to get Ian's autograph too, after I told him that I was a red-hot Liverpool F.C. supporter.

Another amazing event happened while I was on a business trip to Tampa, Florida. I was walking out of the Hilton Hotel toward the front of the building, where I was to be picked up and taken to dinner. As I approached the front of the hotel, I noticed a man standing there with his back toward me, head buried in a newspaper. What made me notice him in particular was the size of his thighs, which looked like those of the Incredible Hulk just before he burst out of his clothes.

We stood alongside each other, and I thought he also appeared to be waiting for a pickup. A taxi then pulled up and out got a man who, after paying off the cabbie, turned to walk into the hotel. On seeing my muscular companion, he dropped his suitcases and asked the man for his autograph. It turned out that he was the famous Cincinnati Reds baseball player, Pete Rose, and in his sport was just as famous as George Best was to soccer. His nickname was "Charlie Hustle," and he was revered throughout the sport of baseball. He gave the guy his autograph, and turning to me, he asked if I would like his autograph also. I said that I would and began to chat with him. He then asked me where I was from.

Instead of telling him Britain, being a bit mischievous, I said, "Detroit."

"Oh, you're one of Sparky's boys," he answered, referring to his ex-coach, "Sparky" Anderson, who'd left the Cincinnati Reds and was now coaching the Detroit Tigers. "Look at this," Pete said pointing to the newspaper, "The seventh dog race at Hialeah, it's 'Sparky's Girl.' I guess I'll place a bet on this dog on the strength of our chance meeting."

His lift came first, and he left bidding me a cheerful "So long." When my lift arrived a few minutes later, he was chagrined to think that he'd missed the great Pete Rose by such a short time. A few months later, Pete Rose was banned from ever playing baseball again because— —it was alleged— —he had been caught betting on the result of baseball games. Even though he insisted that he never bet on any game that he had played or coached in, the baseball commission came down on him hard. Pete was a shoe-in for the Baseball Hall of Fame, but because of his betting addiction, he'll never be inducted. I sure hope that Sparky's Girl won for him that night.

Unfortunately, some years later, when I was hurting for money, I was silly enough to sell Pete Rose's autograph. I regret it to this day.

On another occasion, I was taking a business associate to catch a flight out of Detroit Metropolitan Airport. When we got to the gate, the whole Boston Red Socks baseball team was waiting to catch the same flight to Toronto. My guy was going on to Britain, but the Sox were going to play the Blue Jays. I don't remember all of their names but some of the more famous players were Jim Rice, Carlton Fisk, Denis Eckersley, Butch Hobson, and Fred Kendall.

I was idly chatting with Jerry Remey when he said, "You guys play cricket and catch a ball with your bare hands, right? No mitt?"

He told me that he had been playing in a baseball game once, when a fly ball had been hit to center field. It was quite windy, and the outfielder was running with his mitted left-hand outstretched when the wind drifted the ball away and behind him. He stuck out his un-mitted right hand behind him and snagged the ball barehanded. Jerry told me that, in all his years in baseball, this was the one and only time he had ever witnessed such a catch.

Traveling around America was a great adventure, as I was either seeing great places or meeting great people. Once on the outskirts of St. Louis, Missouri, I met another baseball great named Stan Musial. I was having dinner at the Chase Park Plaza hotel when a guy approached my table to inquire if everything was to my satisfaction.

When he'd departed, a gentleman at the next table leaned over and said, "Hey, bud, that's 'Stan the Man.'" Then he went on to tell me Stan's life's history, which was way too much to take in at one time. He was now part owner of this fine restaurant and seemed to be enjoying himself having left the sports life behind.

Some other people of note that I met on my travels were Hulk Hogan (wrestler), Merlene Otley (Jamaican Olympic sprinter), Eric Hipple (quarterback for the Detroit Lions), Mickie Redmond (ex-Detroit Red Wings hockey great), Allan Ball (1966 World Football Cup player), and Carlos Valdarama (Columbian soccer player with two World Cups under his belt).

Fourteen
The Traveling

On the work front, I had completed the two years with Kean Mfg. We shook hands and parted company on the day they handed me my green card. I will always be indebted to those ladies, particularly Sally Snyder and Peggy Campbell, for giving me the opportunity to stay and work in the U.S.

Within two weeks, I started a new job at Universal Engineering out of Frankenmuth, Michigan. For those of you who've never visited this town, it is a German-style town known for its Christmas gift shops, open all year round, and its chicken dinners sold out of two huge restaurants owned by the Bronner family. As Universal's sales manager, covering the automotive industry, I began the week by driving up to Frankenmuth for the weekly management meeting. During the winter, this was quite an ordeal because before the sun came up in the morning, the roads were often covered in ice and extremely slick. I spun off the road on one such morning and ended up in a roadside ditch. I sat there for a moment catching my breath, and then I decided that the ground was perhaps so frozen that it might be hard enough to support the weight of my car. I ran the car along the ditch, with two wheels on one side of the ditch and two wheels on the other and then yanked the steering wheel with just enoughmomentum to get the car back onto the road.

On another occasion, on pulling off the motorway at the Frankenmuth exit, the off-ramp was completely iced over. I hit my brakes as I was approaching the intersection, but nothing happened! I went sailing straight across the road, between the traffic, and back down the on-ramp on the other side of the intersection! Whew!

While working for this company, my family and I took a vacation and traveled down to Nashville and Memphis, Tennessee, to see the Grand Ole Opry and Graceland, the home of Elvis Presley. I also went to the Loraine Motel to see the spot where Martin Luther King was assassinated.

I also took a paddleboat ride on the mighty Mississippi River. At the Grand Ole Opry, Roy Acuff and his usual band of characters were there on the stage, and he introduced "a little lady named Skeeter Davis." For your information, the people from that state call mosquitoes skeeters, and she was called this on account of her being so small, but what a huge voice came out of that little lady.

At Graceland it was an eerie experience to stand over the grave of Elvis. I was not a big fan of his, but I had to agree that just like the Beatles, he had made his mark on his particular music genre, and you had to respect that. We also drove over to the Smokey Mountains, and at the town of Cherokee, North Carolina, we saw our first full-blooded American Indian. From there, we went through the Smokeys to Gatlinburg and Pigeon Forge, the home of Dolly Parton. This was the center of the country music of the mid-south and, of course, the Bluegrass music of Ketucky and Tennessee. It is said that the music of this area is a mixture of Irish music and sea-shanties, and the main instruments at the heart of it all are the fiddle, the banjo, and the squeezebox (piano accordion).

For my jazz-loving friends, I have three stories which should strike a note of some significance. On a business trip to Chicago, the "Windy City," I was at a trade show when I received an invitation to a party later that evening at a circular-shaped apartment building. This building is the only structure to the east of Lake Shore Drive, and the event was being hosted by a public relations company. The party was good; there was plenty of booze and good food, and I happened to glance out of the window and down to a tickertape billboard advertising that evening's entertainment at a nearby hotel. I could not believe what I'd just seen, so I asked the hostess if she by chance had a pair of binoculars. She did and brought them to me.

Adjusting them so I could read the billboard better, I read, "One Night Only: Stan Getz." Now this gentleman was considered by many jazz fans to be the purest tenor saxophone player in the business. I left the party abruptly and soon found myself in the lounge of the Holiday Inn. As we sat down — —several of the partygoers had left with me— —Mr. Getz announced that the evening's entertainment was now over. A waitress was just passing, and I asked her for pen and paper. I scribbled off a quick note and asked her to pass it to Mr. Getz. He read the note, and looking straight at me announced that he would play just one more set for a "jazz fan from England." The crowd was in rapture, and after the set was over, I went up to the stage and thanked him for his kindness. Of course, I got his autograph.

He looked me in the face and in a gruff voice— —he was suffering from and later died of throat cancer— —he said, "Any friend of Ronnie Scott's is a friend of mine." What a wonderful man!

On a visit to the northwest area of Chicago, I was staying at the Hilton Hotel just outside Arlington Park Race Track. I came down to the bar around 8:00 p.m. to find a mighty fine traditional jazz band blowing up a storm. At a break in the music, the bandleader, a clarinetist, came over to the bar, and I told him right out that his band was great. After a few minutes of conversation, I asked him who his drummer was because he seemed to have a rare quality about his style.

Before replying, the bandleader first asked me, "Who

do you think are the top five drummers of all time?" I began to list, "Gene Krupa, Buddy Rich, etc., etc."

He said that I was on the right track, but this guy was the only white drummer to play for Louis Armstrong. Immediately, I said, "Barrett Deams!" Well, this was he! It was the same guy who played with "Satchmo" in the film *High Society*.

Barrett came over, and we talked until he had to go back to the stage. I had a flashback to my old pal, Trevor Roberts, imitating Satchmo, "Now you hazz jazz," he would sing, "and now you have Mr. Barrett Deams," as he broke into an imaginary drum solo.

My last little "jazzy" story is concerning a visit I made to New Orleans, the "Big Easy." Obviously, I had to visit Bourbon Street. I worked my way from bar to bar, carrying my drinks with me as is the custom, until I was standing outside Preservation Hall. It was so small that only about fifty people at a time could enter. Finally, I was sitting on a straight-backed chair facing six men whose average age had to be in the high seventy- to eighty-year-old range. They all sat in a line facing the audience, and between them and us was a brass spittoon.

Nothing happened until I suddenly realized that they weren't going to play anything until somebody threw some bread into their tip jar. I stood up and walked over to the spittoon, and waving a twenty-dollar bill, I shouted as loud as I could, "When the Saints Go Marching In."

They immediately responded with some of the best music I've ever heard, and the rest of the crowd went wild. The room went from total silence to total anarchy in two seconds flat. What an experience! I shall carry that memory to my grave!

On my first business trip to Los Angeles, I stopped at a coffee bar just off Figaroa Street at around 10:00 a.m. I was sitting there sipping my Java when into the café came a group of four or five punk rockers. They had the usual brightly colored Mohawk hairstyles and the compulsory leather jackets festooned with chains. They stood just inside the door of the café but never made any attempt to order drinks or food and quite honestly, apart from their appearance, they were acting way too refined for any rockers that I had ever witnessed. They grouped together muttering in low tones and kept peering out the door as if they were expecting something significant to happen. Then suddenly, as quickly as they had come, they left leaving me with a decidedly odd feeling.

I approached the cash register to pay for my drink and mentioned to the barman the unusual sequence of events that had just taken place, and I asked him what he made of it.

"Mike Hammer," he said with a deadpan expression, leaving me no better informed. I walked out through the same door as my punk friends had and in so doing walked right onto the street set of the television detective series of the same name. Immediately someone on the set asked me to go back into the café and exit through the side door, which I had originally come in by, which led to another street around the corner. Because of this, I decided to buy another cup of joe and stick around to see what would happen next. I could observe the street set through a nearby window and watch them film a few scenes when someone shouted, "Take a break, gang."

At this time the door opened again and in walked Stacey Keach who played the title role of Mike Hammer.

I asked Stacey for his autograph and engaged him in some small talk. He was very pleasant, and I asked him what he thought of English prisons. The significance of this question was that he had spent several days in an English jail after being stopped at Heathrow Airport, London, and was arrested for having marijuana in his possession.

He smiled, winked, and said, "Not so bad, kid." He was kind of amused by the fact that I was aware of his predicament, because it had hardly ever been reported upon by the American news media.

Because of this encounter, I began watching the Mike Hammer series, and about four months later, I had the pleasure of seeing the episode that I was almost a part of. Ray Milland would have been proud.

Fifteen
The Tipperary

About this time, I opened up a sports retail store specializing in soccer equipment. It was on Schafer Road in East Dearborn, and I shared the space with Jean Greenan and Rose Quigley, two Scottish ladies who had a hairdressing business in the rear.

With all my contacts in the various leagues and clubs, business was good. Through Jean and Rose, I met Dave McKay, who was president of the local Scottish club, the "White Heather." He was told that someone from the Detroit Express had invited a youth team from Kilmarnock (Ayrshire, Scotland) to visit Michigan as their guest. The Express contacted David, who panicked, and then came to me asking if I could possibly host these young soccer players through the Dearborn Youth Soccer Club. The people of Dearborn were great in their response and rose to the task brilliantly. The Killie Colts arrived on a two-week visit, played soccer, and made friends in America.

The next year, John Bricknell and I took our youth team over to Scotland for a two-week visit. This happened, back and forth, for a further two visits before it fizzled out.

One incident that sticks in my mind was the day we all took a boat ride on Loch Lomond, just outside Glasgow

67

(Scotland). We had just returned to the dock when there was a loud splash. Looking over the side of the boat, I could see a young nude American boy in the Loch. It was Robert Pruzinski, and I asked him whatever possessed him to do such a thing because the water temperature was down around fifty degrees. Robert's answer was that his father had asked him, if he ever got the opportunity, to take a dip for him in Loch Lomond. Apparently, it had always been his father's dream to do so!

Roughly two years later, I had to change my job again having been released by Universal Engineering because of a general business slump throughout the automotive industry. Within a month, I was working for TM Smith, a company that competed with Universal and made the same product line.

Fred Smith, the owner, was the second millionaire that I had worked for, Mr. Norman Moore being the first. What a difference, though! Mr. Norman Moore mixed with the upper crust of British society, while Fred carried a gun, a big wad of cash, had a fast speedboat called Quick Change, and loved to play pinball machines. They were as different as chalk and cheese.

All this time I was running my sports store (called Metro Tri-County Sports Supply) and was still the city of Dearborn's soccer director. I was also still vice president of the Dearborn Soccer Club and president of the Great Lakes Youth Soccer League, was coaching two teams, and was actually playing myself for the Tipperary Rovers. The Tipperary pub, owned by Tommy O'Halloran, was our sponsor and home base for post-game parties.

One Sunday after a game, we all piled into the Tip (as we normally did), and, in fact, I was in charge of the beer kitty. There was Bobby Harrison, Billy Dixon, Jimmy Hill, Jimmy Craig, Jim Kelly, Ralph McNulty, Seamus McCallion, Jamie McCracken, and the rest of our motley crew.

All of a sudden, a load of pitchers of beer was brought over to us by Pete, the barman. I protested, saying that I hadn't ordered them and that he was getting ahead of himself. He told me not to worry as they had been bought and paid for by the young man at the far end of the bar.

Peering through the gloom in that direction, I could just make out a sharp-faced, spiky-haired man sitting with two very attractive young ladies. I sauntered down the bar to thank him, and, my God, it was Rod Stewart! No one else was in the bar, just him, his friends, and the soccer team. Each of us had a quick chat with him, and so did Tommy O'Halloran, when he came in.

A funny story is that Tommy ran into Rod some years later at the Irish Grand National, and without breaking a smile Tommy said, "Are you following me?" to which Rod just beamed and winked.

One of the Scottish members of the Tipperary soccer team, we'll call him "Blue," was always causing problems with his anti-Catholic rhetoric. He was a Glasgow Rangers fan and didn't care who knew it. He took great delight in ribbing the Glasgow Celtics fans at every conceivable opportunity if their team had a bad result or bad news. Unfortunately, Blue's father passed away, and his mother asked him to fly the ashes (he had been cremated) to Scotland and scatter them on Loch Lomond. Like a dutiful son he packed his bags and set off for Detroit Metro Airport. However, he had an hour to kill so, being Blue, he decided to drop in at the Tipperary for a good-bye drink. After saying farewell to everyone, he strode out into the parking lot to find that his car and his father's ashes were gone. Luckily he had his money and airline tickets in his pocket, so he was able to complete his trip. He returned and told his mother that he had done as she requested.

To this day--and this happened some thirty years ago--the mystery has never been solved. Whether it was some fiendish Fennian plot or whether the Lord interceded after all the bad things Blue said about the pope, we will never know. This was an extremely sensitive subject, and no one got on Blue's case, although a lot of behind-the-back comments circulated for many years. The conjecture is that when Blue finally arrives at heaven's door, there will be a great deal of explaining to be done, and his father — — God rest his soul — — has every right to be asking the questions.

Another guy that I made friends with around this time was Dennis Robins, who played guitar and banjo for a band called The Rockets. Their claim to fame was that they toured with, and opened the shows for, Bob Seeger and the Silver Bullet Band. Bob Seeger, a Michigan-born singer with a raspy voice, is now extremely famous throughout America, but to the best of my knowledge, he does not tour outside of the U.S. He is famous for such songs as: "Old Time Rock and Roll," "Hollywood Nights," and "Turn the Page."

Another side story is that my current wife, Sharon, used to work at an all-night diner named "Flags," right off I-94 at Belleville. Every Saturday night, for several years, Bob Seeger and his band would step in for their breakfast in the early hours of what would then be Sunday morning. They would always ask to be seated in her section, and at the tender age of eighteen or nineteen, she was obviously flattered. However, just like me with the Beatles, she never once asked for their autographs, as she didn't want to invade their privacy. If she had known then that they'd become world famous, she might have asked.

One snowy winter's night, I came out of the Tipperary and proceeded to leave the parking lot in my car. The road, which is the south service drive for the Southfield Freeway, was iced so bad that I lost control of the car and ended up in a snow bank at the side of the road. I went back into the bar and asked for some assistance, and just inside the front door stood Jim Brandstetter. Jim was a huge man who was once a star University of Michigan football player and was now an announcer for a local Detroit TV sports channel. I was hoping for three or four helpers, but all it took was Jim. With me and a passenger in the car, he lifted the front end and walked with it in his hands and placed it back onto the road. This took all of about ten seconds, and every time I bumped into Jim and his newscaster wife, Robbie Timmings, he would ask how my car was doing. I have never experienced such brute strength before in my lifetime, and I don't think he even got his hands dirty.

Sixteen
The Game

Back in the old country, I played rugby for twenty-five years — — eight in Wales and seventeen in England. In America, I played soccer for another twenty-five years. Throughout all my jobs and my travels, sport was the one constant. I played for the Tipperary Rovers, which then became the "Stroh's team" because one of our players, Tom Carey, played the bagpipes for the Stroh's Brewery Scottish Band and somehow was able to siphon off some of their funds to buy us uniforms and beer. The same team and players, then moved on to be sponsored by some bar up on Warren Avenue, which was arranged by Jimmy Craig. When that money ran out, we moved again to a bar up on Seven Mile Road, which was arranged by Noel McCall. When that deal fell through, we got sponsored by the Dearborn Tavern and then the Falls Lounge, both in Dearborn. Finally we ended up playing for some bar up on the Pontiac Trail, arranged by Peter Notini.

To say we were "soccer whores" was a mild understatement. Basically we would play for any bar within a twenty-mile radius of our home field, so long as they bought us uniforms and gave us ten pitchers of beer to start the postgame party. Now, a lot of bars were willing to do this,because we played our games on a Sunday afternoon, normally hit thebar at 5:00 p.m., and stayed for a good five or six hours. This time-slot was perfect for the bar owner, as it was usually a slow customer time. Our being there brought loads of others in to watch our antics and to hear the latest stories of our bravado on the field of combat.

When I finished my playing time with the Whore Rovers, in the over-30 bracket, I then moved on to play for the Ferndale Internationals for three or four years. This meant, however, that even my home games were an hour's drive away. Finally, when Canton Celtics entered a team into the same Michigan United League, I jumped ship so that I wouldn't have to travel so far. All the players on the Celtics team came out of Canton Soccer Club's in-house Sunday League, so I virtually knew them all — — such guys as Hugh Lindsay, Mostyn Connor, Art Gastewicz, Wayne Colozinsky, Rick Wilkerson, Jerry Mieir, Jimmie Canfield, Mark Belinda, Dan McGary, and various other misfits. I have played against teams from many nations: German, Polish, Croatian, Iraqi, Lebanese, Maltese, Albanian, Macedonian, Armenian, Romanian, Korean, Yugoslavian, West Indian, African, and Greek.

Some of these games were like World War III with no quarter being given and none being asked. In all of those games, which I guess would number around 1,000, I was only, ever, given a red card once. That means, in a combined fifty years of rugby and soccer, I have the distinction of never having been sent off the playing field. Only once, in my last year of playing, did I falter. Not too bad, hey!

Another similarity in the two sports is that, in my last game in both sports, I scored a try, or goal, and retired from the game. I considered that going out on a scoring game was the proper way to hang my boots up.

As I look around my office and see all the team photographs, the trophies, and the hanging boots, the memories come flooding back. I think of the comradeship and the excitement and all the accomplishments. I must have won six or seven league and divisional titles plus five or six knock-out competition cup final trophies.

I mentioned earlier my very good friend, Mostyn Connor. Like me, Mostyn came from Wales and lived in the famous steel-making town of Ebbw Vale. Although my homtown, Pontypool, and his were only about twenty miles apart, we never met until Mostyn and his family moved from Chicago to the Livonia area of Michigan. He and his son, Phillip, both turned up at Bi-Centennial Park trying to hook up with the Livonia Bullets, but they had a full roster. They then crossed over to our bench and asked one of our team (the Whores) if we had room for two more players. I turned up just after this, and having heard a distinct Welsh accent, I went over and introduced myself. We couldn't play them that day because they weren't on our roster, and the Livonia Bullets knew that, but we did sign them up, and they became Roving Whores shortly after.

Now Mostyn, in his younger days back in Wales, was as good at football as I was at rugby and had played with some exceptional teams and some extraordinary players. One of the teams he'd played for had ten ex-professionals on it. Mostyn was the eleventh player, and he was still just a teenager. He was a prolific goal scorer and for that reason was sought out by many teams. Like Bobby Harrison, who missed a chance at a professional football career, so had Mostyn, again, through no fault of his own. The local scout for Chelsea F.C. had picked two boys to go up to London for a trial, which would be every boy's dream. The only snag was that the other boy's father had a car, but Mostyn did not. He was told that he could ride with them and to be at a certain pickup point at a particular time. Well, he was stood up! They never picked him up, but left him standing there like a spare groom at a wedding. The other boy signed a contract with Chelsea; his name was Colin Coats.

Mostyn and I took a trip back to Wales and England about five years ago. We had a really good time. We saw Wales vs. Moldovia, at Cardiff, for the European Cup. We saw Tranmere Rovers vs. Charlton Athletic, at Birkenhead, in the English First Division. We did the tour of Liverpool F.C.'s home ground at Anfield, and even had a photograph taken in the home team's changing room wearing actual players' jerseys! I was wearing Neil Ruddock's, and Mostyn was wearing Michael Owen's.

We were staying in West Kirby, on the Wirral in Cheshire, and Mostyn needed to exchange some traveler's checks for cash, so we went down to the local bank. It was almost closing time, and since he was just going to pop in, do the deal, and pop out again, I parked right in front of the bank in a no-parking zone. About twenty minutes went by, and there was still no Mostyn, when two police cars came tearing up and came to a screeching halt alongside my car. I was thinking that I was about to be taken to jail, when all the policemen poured out of their paddy wagons and dashed into the bank.

Then I was thinking it was Mostyn who was going to jail, as he could get quite belligerent if he was not catered to immediately. When he finally came out, he explained to me that, as he entered the bank, the manager came up and asked him to step into his office. Once there, the manager explained that the man standing in front of Mostyn at the teller's window was on a wanted list for passing bad checks. The police had been notified and were on their way to pick him up.

We didn't get any reward for assisting in the arrest, but the story did get us some free beers in the pubs around West Kirby for a few days!

Another funny incident happened when we went to Abergavenny Market (South Wales) for a day out. We popped into a pub right across from the livestock yards and put in an order for our lunch at the bar. As was the custom, we paid for the meal, and seeing an opening for two seats, we moved away from the bar. We'd ordered a very Welsh concoction called "faggots and peas." Faggots are savory meatballs served with green peas boiled to mush in a bowl of hot gravy. About ten minutes went by when out of the kitchen came a woman with two steaming hot bowls on a tray. She stopped and was clearly looking around for us. I seized the opportunity to get a rise out of Mostyn and shouted, "Two faggots over here!" You could have heard a pin drop in the pub! From the corner of his mouth, Mostyn replied, "You arsehole!"

I took this as a compliment from a man who used to refer to his own son as "Shit for Brains."

Seventeen
The Betrayal

Two more years went by, and I was now working for the Illinois Tool Works, Eclipse Division, as their national sales manager. This was a good, medium-sized company producing specialized cutting tools, and although they weren't setting the world on fire, they were profitable. For reasons known only to the board of ITW, they decided to sell this and a sister company in Arkansas off to a group of investment bankers out of St. Louis.

ITW were now heavily into producing plastic products, so I guess cutting tools were no longer fashionable enough for them to stay involved. The whole thing was a fiasco and stank very heavily of what can only be called extreme bad judgment. However, ITW was out and the bankers— —some never-before-heard-of holding company— —were in.

We all got the "nothing is going to change" speech, but that meant, basically, they'd keep Eclipse for as long as it would take for them to take an inventory of all the machinery and equipment before what was to become an asset-stripping operation. How I hated those investment bankers!

It was obvious from the beginning that they had no interest in running the plant as a going concern. Well, I worked for them and took their money, but, frankly, I was disgusted and spent considerably more time than usual at my retail sporting goods business. They finally, as they politely say, let me go but not before I had gotten all I needed for my own advancement. I did not mind this one bit, but what I did resent was that they closed the whole plant, putting some 150 good people on the streets. This was capitalism at its worst!

I was so sickened by the whole incident that, after some thirty-odd years, I left the engineering field completely and worked full time at my sporting goods business. Although the money was nowhere near as good, my peace of mind was greatly enhanced. My business allowed me to completely immerse myself in the game of soccer, from Pee Wees right up to the professional level. The first Detroit Express team had folded, but some new owners revived it under the same name although on a less-grand scale in the American Soccer League. A whole new bunch of players came along, such as Brian Tinnion, Gus Moffet, Andy Chapman, Pato Majestic, Clyde Watson, Arnie Majalovik, Billy Bolevich, and many more.

The main difference between this team and its predecessor was the fact that the rules had changed. The majority of the players were now American-born or new American citizens, and only four players could be outside of those categories. Again, because the NSL had collapsed, a new league was in charge, so a whole lot of new teams sprung up, and I was able to meet many more new visiting players. The new Express again played at the Pontiac Silverdome, and, again, the post-game parties were at the Main Event restaurant within that building.

I was now mixing with visitors such as Mike English, Billy Ronson, Ray Hudson, Charlie Cooke, and many more. At the same time, I was making a lot of contacts for my own sporting goods supply business.

On one deal, I sold seventy pairs of soccer shoes to a visiting team from Romania, all paid for by their U.S. hosts, the Dearborn Stars, a Lebanese team. I also supplied gloves to the Livonia Wolftones, who went to San Francisco and came back as All-American Gaelic League champions. As it happened, on the day of the final, it rained heavily and the gloves, which incidentally I gave to them, became an integral part of the victory. As soon as the Tones got back into town, their captain, Jimmy O'Shaunessey, and the Murray brothers, brought the Cup in, and I displayed it in my shop window. Those were good times, and out of the ten years that I owned the store, the first eight were profitable. The last two, alas, became so bad that I finally had to pull the plug on it.

The huge American retailers like Sports Giant finally got into the soccer supply business, and I could quite honestly buy items at their stores, double the price, and still make a good profit. At this time, the major goods suppliers like Adidas, Puma, Nike, and Umbro, sold us small stores, who'd opened up the market for them, down the river. I finally had to liquidate my business, sell my house, and file for bankruptcy. Not a very nice situation!

Before the final closing of my store, I had already moved more than half of my inventory to a local dealers' mall, so when the doors were finally locked, I was already set up for business again. All in all, I did end up losing around $40,000, but I began a mail-order business out of my new apartment while selling off the rest of my stock from the mall on the weekends. I did this for about one year, and when the mall was closed down because the owner reneged on his rent, I moved my goods out and sold them at an outdoor flea market on the weekend. Unlike the mall, where I could leave my goods all set up throughout the week, at the flea market I had to set up and break down each day.

On the plus side, however, there were many more people at the outdoor market. By the end of another year, two in all, I had recouped the $40,000 I'd lost. I had now broken even. Now that all this messing about was over, after twelve years I was totally out of the sporting goods supply business. On the upside, I had now experienced the most difficult type of sales of all and the toughest period of my life.

The retail business has two major stumbling blocks: the sheer unpredictability of the general public and the almost equal unpredictability of the suppliers' new product introduction. In other words, just when you think you're in complete control of the situation, everything changes. Last year's models are now no longer trendy, and with mass advertising, particularly on television, customers are at your door even before the new goods have hit the shelves. As a little company, as soon as you've caught up with all the new trends, another year has gone by, and the whole cycle begins again.

In my career, I've sold many things, in many ways, but retailing has got to be one of the worst. I can only think of one other method of sales which has possibly got to be more soul-destroying: door-to-door. Meeting a customer on his or her own turf— —the home— —having to carry your samples everywhere, and then having to persuade people that they cannot live without whatever the product is must require the patience of Job. Anyone who's been successful in this field has my total admiration.

Mark, my daughter's significant other, is just such a person, and although he has his quirks— —he refuses to work any nine-to-five job— —in his field he is quite brilliant!

Eighteen
The Greatest

In 1994, the World Football Cup came to America, and the Detroit area was one of eight cities selected for first-round matches. Here again, I seized the initiative, and for the three months leading up to the event and for the two weeks of the actual games, I sold my own designed and printed T-shirts.

During my many years in the sports industry, I had to supply various shirts individually designed for specific teams, clubs, and organizations. To do this, I worked very closely with various silk-screening companies, and once again, I was able to work with them. Some shirts and hats I bought complete from original manufacturers, but others I designed and had printed locally.

I made up a generic shirt, to celebrate the event, but I also had another style of shirt that had the same design throughout. Then the national colors were introduced to suit each separate country with the country's name beneath the design. I concentrated on those countries scheduled to play at the Pontiac Silverdome. They were U.S., Switzerland, Brazil, Sweden, Russia, and Romania. I also had the same shirt made up for teams playing at other locations, if those countries had ethnic supporters living in the Detroit area. I selected countries like Italy, Germany, Greece, Mexico, Spain, and Ireland.

These nationals owned a lot of restaurants, pubs, and clubs in and around the Detroit area. The whole event was a great success.

I also sold my wares at a popular Pontiac watering hole called the Ultimate Sports Bar, where several of the World Cup players came to relax after the games. I met some of the Swedish team players such as Martin Brolin, Kennet Andersson, and Martin Dahlin. The Swiss team with Alain Sutter and Stephan Henchoz, plus the U.S. team with Alexi Lalas and Joe Max-Moore also came in. I was lucky enough to meet them all.

One slight hiccup in the whole joyous occasion was the fact that I was paid a visit by the FBI who told me to cease and desist in the selling of my goods because they were not authorized goods. Apparently, their rule was that non-authorized goods could not be sold within two miles of the stadium at which the games were being played. I argued that the Ultimate Sports Bar was exactly 2.1 miles from Pontiac Silverdome. At that, the feds produced a map of the city of Pontiac, which had a two-mile circle (from the stadium) drawn on it. The bar fell just within the circle, but because it was a borderline case, they didn't confiscate my inventory.

This incident didn't hamper me too much as it was on the evening of the last game between Brazil and Sweden, and I was almost completely sold out anyway. All in all, I sold around $52,000 over that period, and for quite a number of years afterwards, I could still see my personally designed shirts being worn all over that area. This gave me a real sense of satisfaction.

I phoned my good friend Pete Morrell back in Wales and suggested that he ought to jump on the first available flight and come over for the event. I had already gone to the opening match between the U.S. and Switzerland, which had ended in a one-to-one tie. Four days later, I was at Detroit Metro Airport to meet Pete as he flew in from the UK. He arrived at about 6:00 p.m., and since Metro was on the south-west side of Detroit and Pontiac was on the northeast side, there was no way we could make the 7:00 p.m. kickoff for the second game between Romania and Switzerland. I drove Pete straight to a bar in Livonia, called the Yacht Club, and we sat on the deck overlooking the lake and watched the game on TV. We did, however, get tickets for the Sweden vs. Russia game plus tickets for my son, Richard, and his wife, Laura.

Pete and I were also able to get tickets for the last game at Pontiac, and we saw the great Romario score a magnificent goal for Brazil against Sweden.

About five years later, Pete returned the courtesy by getting me two tickets to see South Africa play New Zealand, at Cardiff, at the World Rugby Cup. This game was on a Thursday evening and was for the third-place team as they'd both been beaten by Australia and France respectively.

Before the game, my wife and I were at the Angel Hotel directly across the street from the Millennium Stadium having a drink with some "Boks" fans. They called another guy over, and he turned out to be the backs' coach for the Springbok team. I reminded him that whoever lost that night would have to re-qualify for the next tournament in four years' time. I also stressed the fact that the presence of Jonah Lomu was a possible threat.

This guy's name was Andy Solomon, and his reply was, "Jonah has never scored a try against us, and he will not tonight. We will win!"

Well, true to his word, Jonah did not score, and, yes, South Africa did win! I now know where the saying, "As wise as Solomon" comes from.

That night, I enjoyed a celebratory drink with ex-prop Barnie Swart and ex-lock JD Schmidt. These two players had, in fact, won the World Rugby Cup four years earlier while playing for their host nation, South Africa.

It would be remiss of me if I did not mention the good people of Newport Saracens RUFC. Every time I've revisited East Gwent, whether at their club or at the Red Lion (Leon

Rouge) at Caerleon, their hospitality has been unequaled. The likes of Mark and Ivor Thom, Arthur Young, the Clode brothers, Johnnie Richards, John and Mike Shine, and the lovely, lovely late Bob Vickery have brought joy to my heart. The parties at the Angel in Cardiff, where I met people like Gareth Edwards, JPR Williams, Mervin Davies, and Gerald Davies— —all at the height of their careers— —will never be forgotten. The trips to the St. Pierre Golf Club with Arthur singing "Buddy Can You Spare a Dime?" while propped up on two up-ended brooms cannot be topped. It seemed that, no matter where I met these people, they were the center of activity. With them I've heard the Treorchy Male Voice Choir, together with a few females, sing "Myfanwy," which made chills run up and down my spine.

I also met them in Atlanta, Georgia, when they were visiting the U.S. as guests of the Renegades. The Saries had selected and rehearsed an American song, in honor of their hosts. Mark Thom called for attention, and a hush fell over the room. At his prompting, the Welshmen, very seriously, launched into a well-rehearsed version of "John Brown's Body," not knowing it was a song of the Yankee North. Without prompting, the Gades each stood individually, and over the top of "John Brown's Body," they began to sing "The Battle Hymn of the Republic." For a totally off-the-cuff happening, the effect was truly amazing! I've not heard anything at the Albert Hall that could compare with that evening. That night, the term "Gochy Da Y'all" was born.

Last, but not least, the story of the Sary member, who was involved in coercing certain, very famous, players to allow him to enter the Welsh team's dressing room and paint three white stripes on their (obviously) non-Adidas boots, will go down in the legends of the game of rugby. The shear audacity of it shows that these people think outside the box.

Nineteen
The Obsession

My two off-field obsessions are crossword puzzles and bar pool. Since there is not too much that can be said for the excitement of crosswords, let's talk about pool.

As a young teenager growing up in Pontypool, I began playing billiards and snooker in the rooms underneath the Park Cinema. I would also watch the older men play for money, small though it was.

I remember watching a little oriental guy called Jacko playing his artful game. He was left behind by a travelling troupe in which he was a comedian. Their version of pool was to set up the snooker balls as for a regular game. In one pocket, they would put six beer bottle tops, on the cork underside of which would be written the numbers two through seven. The first player, in singles or doubles to pot a red ball, would take out one of the bottle caps, take note of the number, but not allow anyone else to know what it was. With yellow ball being two, green three, brown four, blue five, pink six, and black seven, the number would denote his selected ball. To win the game, all he had to do was pot the ball corresponding to the number he'd picked. For example, if the cap was marked five, the blue ball was his.

As the other player or players picked a bottle cap, they

all had object balls to try to pot. It was a cat-and-mouse game with each player trying not to give his number away before he could pot it. If any of the other players potted someone else's ball, by good deduction or pure dumb luck, he was out of the game. The winner, having potted his ball first, would take the money. I have seen a lot of money change hands in this Welsh (or Pontypool) version of pool.

Years after coming to America, I began playing the different versions of American pool, being eight-ball, nine-ball, or last pocket. I did fairly well at first, mainly because the pockets on an American pool table are almost twice the size as those of a British billiard table. As my reputation began to grow, the pool sharks began to circle, and before too long, I was being given some severe beatings and losing some serious money.

The good American pool players have three very powerful assets. The first is that they can eye up a table from the break and reading the lie of each ball, they know immediately whether to shoot at solids or stripes or, as they would say, little ones or big ones.

The second asset is that good players have learned how to position the cue ball after each shot to make their next shot as easy as possible. If they do this eight times in a game, they can run all their balls off the table without the opposition even taking a shot.

The third asset is their power-breaks at the start of each game which very often give them a ball down off the break, and they can, with very good breaks, pot the eight ball and finish the game before it starts.

These were the aspects of American pool that I had to master if I was going to be able to play and, hopefully, beat the better players. They would often taunt, "If you can't run with the big dogs, stay on the porch."

It took me many hours of playing to get on a par with these guys, only to find that out there were even better classes of players who played in organized leagues and who were handicapped according to their skill level.

I eventually plucked up enough courage to join a traveling team that played for a local bar in the Budweiser League. The handicaps went from one to seven (seven being the best). You would begin as a four handicap and go up, or down, as determined by the results of your first four weeks' games. The teams consisted of eight members, but only five could play in any one match. Team rosters were handed in before the first game was played so that each team captain could weigh up the opposing teams' handicaps before deciding which team members he would use that night.

The toss would be made, and each team would pick their first match players. The team that won the toss would allow the losing team to nominate their player, and then the winning team, with the advantage, would nominate their player for that match.

Say the losing team put their big gun up first, their seven handicap; then the toss-winning team had to decide if they should use their top player or put in a lower handicapped player. This sequence would be repeated for all five games, but the break would be decided by both players lagging.

Each of the two players softly shot the cue ball down the table hitting the rail at the far end, to make the ball come back to the starting rail. The nearest to the rail (cushion) won the break.

Two other interesting and different rules were that the cue ball, on being shot at the object ball and hitting that ball, one or the other of those balls had to hit a rail to prevent players nestling the cue ball against the other. The other rule that differed was that any infraction of the rules by any one player gave "ball in hand" to his opponent. This meant that he could replace the ball on the table at whatever position he felt was the most advantageous for him.

It would take three to four hours to play five pool games as each player had one minute between each shot. The player also had three time outs during each game, when he could confer with his team captain. If any other team member had advice for their player, it had to be passed to the player via the captain. This was playing pool, under pressure in complete silence, and this was fantastic training for playing tournament games.

After two years of playing in the Budweiser League, I was confident enough to play in tournaments. As an explanation of how much my game and concentration had improved, in my first tournament I got to the semis. In the quarter final my opponent won the lag in both games, in a best of three format, and ran all his balls off the table leaving the eight ball right on the pocket.

In both games I slowly, and deliberately, took my time and made certain that I made each individual ball bringing the cue ball off the rail back into the middle of the table. From the middle of the table, I had all straight-in easy shots, and one by one I coolly potted each one, even the eight ball, to take both games. My opponent shook my hand and said that he had never been so near to winning, and yet lost, in his entire pool-playing career. I did not win my semi-final game, but at least I was in the money and picked up a cool $200 prize.

Some months later, I was invited to play in a charity tournament for the treatment of cancer. I lost my sister, at just forty-nine years of age, to that horrible disease, so I signed up immediately. I won my first two games and then came up against my third opponent.

As I was preparing for the game, someone came up behind me and whispered, "That's Corn Bread Red."

Now most people have heard of Minnesota Fats and Willie Masconi, but Corn Bread Red was a living legend in the sport of pool. He as born down on the Kentucky-Tennessee state line and was as poor as dirt. He began frequenting pool halls around eight years of age, and by the time he was fourteen, he was beating everyone in a four-state area.

By the time he was twenty years old, the biggest money players from the whole of the U.S. were seeking him out, just like the old gunfighters of the Wild West. Wherever he played, the big money gamblers followed, either giving him stake money for a percentage of his winnings or making bets on him to win or even making side bets on individual shots. Corn Bread Red was the biggest money winner of all times in the game of pool. Fats and Masconi were better known, but always seemed to be conveniently elsewhere when Corn Bread Red came to play.

At the age of seventy, he beat me with balls to spare. He was gracious and gave me an autographed book, which I cherish to this day. When I asked him about his two more famous counterparts, he said, "Those guys couldn't bank a ball; that's why their position play had to be perfect."

For a semi-literate hillbilly boy, he won— —and lost — —more cash money on one shot than most people can win or lose in a lifetime. By playing the game of table pool, he "done OK."

Twenty
The Spice

Around this time, I decided to take Sharon, my then-fiancée, to Cancun, Mexico, for a week's vacation. I had previously gone there with my friend Mostyn Conner and found it to be an ideal spot. It is on the Yucatan Peninsula, which borders on Central America and has the perfect climate, agreeable food, and long, white beaches.

The night before leaving, we went to Jammer's dance bar up on Plymouth and Farmington roads in Livonia (we were living in Michigan at the time). This was a favorite haunt of ours, and it was owned by Jamie Coe (of Jamie and the Gigolos fame) who was a Neil Diamond look-alike who also happened to be a "sing-alike," too. We got back to Sharon's place in Belleville at around 2:00 a.m., and because we had to leave her house at 6:00 a.m., we decided to stay up all night for fear of oversleeping and missing our flight. We flew out of Detroit Metropolitan Airport by 7:30 a.m. and after a nice nap on the plane, we arrived in Cancun ready to party.

We stayed in a nice, Mexican-styled hotel at the Old Cancun end of the coast, in preference to the Strip, which is totally americanized. The Strip has all the trappings of, say, Las Vegas, with Planet Hollywood, the Hard Rock Café, and just about every other well-known American entertainment outlet. This is fine for a lot of people, but for me, when I go to Mexico, I want to live and experience the Mexican lifestyle.

Now if you ever find yourself in the Cancun area, you simply have to go to Perico's. This restaurant/bar is one of the most fun places that I have ever been to. When you approach the bar, you will notice that the barstools all have saddles on them. Yes, real horse saddles with stirrups, reins, and all. They usually have two bands, which alternate with mariachi and marimba music to entertain you. The waiters and waitresses all dress in authentic Mexican clothing, and between serving your meal, they will serenade you and run around doing all sorts of crazy skits. Somewhere during the evening you will find yourself in a Conga line, which will take you outside of the building, and as you reenter, you'll be met at the door by a gentlemen standing on a chair who will pour the finest tequila into your mouth as you pass beneath him. All these wild and exciting antics add up to one of the best nights that money can buy.

On my previous visit to this region, I had been fascinated by the Mayan culture and history, which prevails in these parts. Most of the tall Mexicans in this area are of Spanish descent, but the little Mexicans, between four- and five-feet tall are, in fact, the original natives who inhabited this land before the Spaniards arrived. These, of course, are the Mayans, and just like their northern neighbors, the Aztecs, they were a savage and at the same time cultured race of people. I had already visited one of the famous Mayan cities and temples at Chitzen Itza, which is situated in the middle of the Yucatan. For this trip I selected a different site to visit, called Tulum, which is about forty miles north of the border with Belize.

Sharon and I were picked up at the hotel, and then the coach stopped at various other tourist spots to collect other day-trippers as we proceeded south. At a place called Playa-de-Carmen, the last crowd of anxious sightseers got onto the coach, and off we went to Tulum.

Tulum is situated on a cliff overlooking the Caribbean Sea and has to be one of the most stunningly rugged and beautiful examples of Mayan ruins that I have ever seen. In fact, recently, I have seen it on the television as the backdrop for an advertisement for a suntan product, and it does the product proud.

When we arrived and got off the coach, we were divided into two groups of about twenty people each. It was then that I noticed a young woman, obviously British, and I just had this feeling that I knew her from somewhere, but I just couldn't figure out from where. As the tour of Tulum continued and the two groups crisscrossed each other several times, every time I saw her, the thought of her identity kept nagging at me.

After the tour, which was amazing, we had about twenty minutes to kill, so Sharon and I took a dip in the aqua-blue Caribbean Sea. We then headed back to the coach because we were now to visit a natural water park called Xelja (pronounced "Shell-ha") on our way back north toward Cancun.

Xelja also proved to be a breathtaking experience. It was set in the jungle right next to the coastline and was left, for the most part, in its naturally beautiful state. We were given a map of this location and were left to our own devices and could wander anywhere within the water park.

On one of the paths we came to some large rocks overlooking a lagoon about twenty feet below. Two couples were already at this site when we strolled up. The two men were diving from the rock into the lagoon while their two female companions sat nearby and were watching the activities. There she was again; and as Sharon and I lingered, I got a long, good look at her, and I was even more certain that I knew her from somewhere.

At the end of our two-to-three-hour visit, we were all told to meet back at the coach before leaving for Cancun. Sharon and I arrived back with about twenty minutes to kill, and we were sitting at an outside Tiki bar, each having a nice bottle of Corona. I had mentioned to Sharon that I seemed to know this young lady from somewhere, and almost immediately up to the bar came the very same woman and was now standing literally right next to us. She ordered a drink in a distinctly Yorkshire cum Spanish accent. Immediately I had a flash of brilliance and blurted out, "Spice Girl."

She looked right at us and said, "Mel B, luv," and walked off with her party's drinks. Mel B, a.k.a Scary Spice, was her identity, and I looked at Sharon who was shaking her head in disbelief and said, "I told you so."

Now she didn't look too much like most people would envision her to be from her stage and television appearances. She had no make up on, no flashy clothes, or big boots, so Sharon would not believe that this woman was a Spice Girl until we got back to our hotel at Cancun later that night. Staying at the hotel was a young couple from Leeds, in Yorkshire, and knowing that Mel B was also from this town, I went looking for them. I found them at the poolside bar and told them of the day's events and our encounter with the Spice Girl. The Leeds man asked me three questions: Was she pregnant? Was she with a man? Describe her male companion.

I answered, yes to the first two questions and "a Puerto Rican-looking guy with a shaved head." To this he acknowledged that the woman that I had seen all that day was in fact Mel B. Case closed.

Still to this day, if ever we see the Spice Girls on television, Sharon begrudgingly has to agree that my intuition once again came through.

Names I am not too good with, but after all my years of working as a salesman, I am great at recognizing faces.

Twenty One
The Grind

Back on the work front, I decided, after the World Football Cup, that I'd had just about as much fun as any one man should be allowed and that I had better go back to some serious career planning. I took a job with a small cutting- tool supply house in Melvindale, but the bull crap was way too deep, and I quickly moved on to one of the top three largest tool distribution companies in the engineering sector.

I spent a year with Production Tool, and although I enjoyed my stay, the money was a tad lacking. I knew too that this was not the company that I would spend the next six to seven years with until I could retire. I'd always planned to retire at the age of sixty-two because it seemed to me that the three years, up to the age of sixty-five, appear to be such a strain for people of that age that many developed bad health— —some people even dying during those last few stressful years. I had vowed at an early age that this would not happen to me. I further vowed that when the time came for me to retire, I would already be living in the place of my choice.

With this criterion in mind, I continued to work diligently, but always had my eye open to ensure that no good career moves would pass me by.

A young and aggressive competitor company in the

Detroit area was called J&L Industrial Supply, and I had always respected their work ethic and their flair. The two original owners of the company had both broken away from Production Tool (my company), and in a reasonably short time, they had become a leading player in the U.S. market of tool distribution.

I was visiting a joint customer of both Production and J&L when the buyer, Jim DuFour, told me that their sales manager had just been at his office asking if he could recommend anyone to work for them as a sales rep. I told him that I was interested, so he picked up the phone and dialed his J&L contact, Jerry Tonna. After a short conversation, he handed me the phone to set up an interview. Two weeks later I was working for J&L, and it was so refreshing to be working for a company that was so responsive to my every need. At that time, to get even the simplest things done at Production Tool was like pulling teeth, but with J&L, the merest suggestion of an improvement was implemented with such speed that it would make your head spin.

I had six good years with J&L and made a lot of money while having a ball. I was selling at a furious pace, and the commissions from those sales, on top of my salary, quickly put me back on a good financial footing. The third year with the company I had 150 customers, had sold slightly over $3 million worth of goods, had a 401k program, and had selected to go very aggressive, particularly with technology stocks.

At the same time I was playing the money market, and that also was paying quick dividends. Just before the stock market took an unstoppable dive, I took out all my money (almost $100,000) and almost immediately bought a house in Florida on Anna Maria Island in the Gulf of Mexico. I continued to work in Michigan and still had my apartment in Livonia, but would visit my home in Florida about twice a year.

The more I visited my home in Bradenton Beach, the more I resented having to return to Michigan where I was-finding the winters really brutal. I was still enjoying working for J&L and had been part of the team that opened up two new stocking depots in the St. Louis, Missouri, and Dallas, Texas, areas. I also worked a number of tool shows in Chicago and Detroit, and I also made visits to some of our leading product suppliers for product training. All these perks made the job less humdrum and were nice alternatives from the regular day-to-day grind of the salesman's chores.

I was still playing soccer with the newly formed Canton Celtics over-40 team and still mixed a great deal of fun and excitement into my life to balance out the tediousness of the workingman's lot. However, there were subtle changes occurring within the company, which I picked up on, and if my keen sense of observation was correct, these were going to be changes that I would not enjoy.

J&L was owned by the huge carbide-manufacturing company, Kennametal, headquartered out of Latrobe, Pennsylvania. They decided that they needed J&L to be the largest engineering supply company in the U.S., a title then held by the Manhattan Supply Co. out of Long Island, New York. Kennametal's strategy was to convert J&L to a public company and put them on the New York Stock Exchange. This brought in around $140 million dollars from the purchases of stock by a string of national banks and money houses.

Now with this money in hand, J&L began buying up other smaller supply houses in an effort to amalgamate their sales and boost the J&L market share. Within two years, they had bought seven such companies and paid top dollar in almost every case. Now this in itself was not too bad of a deal, but J&L, instead of allowing these companies to continue to run the way they had become successful, insisted that these seven companies be integrated into the J&L system of operation.

Before they got the first company up and running, they bought the second, then the third, and so on. This meant that they ended up with seven totally disorganized companies, which were not allowed to run in their normal manner and yet not converted to the J&L system. The net re-sult of this strategic blunder was that they all began hemorrhaging sales, and the reason for initially buying them became irrelevant.

Seeing this, the parent company, Kennametal, cleared out some J&L top management and replaced them with their own people, particularly the sales manager. Their new sales manager tried to reconstruct the sales force à la Kennametal and dropped the salesmen's number of accounts from 150 to 100 then to 50 and then began laying off salespeople. This made J&L's sales spiral downward even faster as the laid-off salespeople went to competitor companies and began calling on those dropped accounts that were supposed to be serviced on the phone by inside telemarketing salespeople.

I watched in horror how, through this chain of events, the whole J&L company began to crumble. At that time I had been with them for four years, and it seemed to me as though the rise and fall of the Roman Empire was being repeated. I needed to be away from this whole situation as quickly as possible.

Twenty Two
The Fix

On the notice board in the hallway was posted all the job openings throughout the company. I was idly drinking a cup of coffee and reading the notifications, when I came across one advertising a sales representative position needed for the state of Florida. I could not believe my good fortune, as I wanted out of Michigan so badly that I could taste it. I went to see the sales manager, and he basically told me that it was perfectly all right by him, but I would have to meet with the regional sales manager for the final OK.

That gentleman came to Livonia headquarters for a sales meeting so we got together and had a nice long chat. He rubber-stamped the deal, and within a month, I was driving a U-Haul truck south down I-75 with all our furnishings. Now at this time, I was approximately two years away from my retirement target of sixty-two years. All I had to do was keep my nose clean, keep a low profile, and sit out the rest of my working years. I had now worked for forty-four years of my life and was located where I wanted to be when I retired. I took the moneys from the 401k and the money market and paid off all my debts on my house and cars and still had a nice little nest egg in the bank. Things were going exactly according to plan.

The next two years passed pleasantly. Every road trip that I took, my wife Sharon would travel with me. We would get to our destination early, book into a nice motel, and she would sit by the swimming pool while I went off and did some business transactions. When I returned, we'd take a swim and then go out for a nice dinner, return to the motel, and have a few nightcaps at the poolside tiki bar before retiring for the night. How civilized!

For the next few days, Sharon would go shopping or lay by the pool, while I was working, but the evenings all had the same sequence of events. This was our *modus operandi* for all business trips. We went to Naples, Ft. Lauderdale, Boca Raton, Daytona Beach, Cocoa Beach, Jacksonville, Miami, Orlando, and just about any city of note in Florida excluding the Panhandle. I think our absolute favorite trips were to the town of St. Augustine, which is the oldest continually inhabited city in the contiguous United States and is one of the prettiest spots in the States.

While I was having fun in the sun, I kept hearing horror stories about how J&L was not only laying off salespeople all over the country but was also closing stocking depots. They even closed down the two at St. Louis and Dallas, which only a few years before I had been involved in opening. I kept my head down and just hoped that they had forgotten that I was still on the payroll.

My original regional manager left to join Manhattan Supply Co., and for about six months I had to report to J&L's regional depot at Charlotte, North Carolina. No one there had any outside sales experience, yet all of a sudden they all wanted to tell me how to do my job. I listened, agreed, and then went off and did the same things that just three years earlier had brought in $3 million in sales.

One day I had to report to some guy that I had never heard of in Houston, Texas. Apparently he was a leftover from one of those companies that I told you we had bought and had somehow hung on, by his fingernails, and weathered the storm.

From the get-go, I didn't like this guy, and since I was only six months away from my projected retirement date, I didn't hide the fact. I had used this reverse psychology technique when departing from Goliath so that I could stay in America.

Being a shrewd judge of character, I felt that this could be used again to my advantage over my newly found buddy.

Eventually he couldn't take the disrespect any longer, and one day he flew into Tampa and asked me to meet with him. He was loaded for bear, and I'm sure couldn't wait to give me his good news. As he laid me off, I just sat across the table from him grinning all over my face. He was totally distracted and asked me what it was that I was beaming about. I didn't tell him in detail of how I had maneuvered the whole situation, but I did tell him that his timing was perfect for me, as I had decided that it was time for me to sit back and enjoy my new surroundings.

He looked around and had to agree that the location I had chosen to live was about as perfect as any place could be. Because of the six years of long and loyal service that I had given to J&L, they in return had given me a whole year's severance pay. This I later found out was a much better deal than a lot of other longer-serving employees had been given. About three months later, the man from Houston was also laid off. Never send a boy to do a man's job.

A long time ago, someone had told me that the only one you work for in life is yourself and that you merely hire your talents out to other people. I was also taught, by another, that there's no longer any loyalty from an employer towards his employees. So why then should employees have any loyalty towards employers? Gone are the days when companies supplied their workers with houses to live in, and gone also are the workers who stayed with a company all their lives only to end up with a gold watch. My advice to anyone in today's employment market is to put yourself, and your family, first in every work-related decision you have to make. In other words, you should say to yourself, *If I do this for the company, how will my family and I benefit in the long run?*

Believe me, when a new manager comes into the company where you're employed, all the sacrifices you've made for that company in the past mean zip, zilch, nada to him. He will fire you as unapologetically as the guy next to you who has done absolutely nothing for the company. When heads have to roll, it is done on a purely statistical and non-emotional basis, and very often it is the accountants (bean counters) who actually make the decision and not the manager of that specific department. So never feel guilty about not going that extra yard for the company because extra yards are not a statistic that a bean counter keeps on his spreadsheet.

When I embarked on my career forty-six years ago, accountants were people who kept the score, and all the others on the team were the people who achieved the score. The CEOs back then had sales or engineering or some other background, but today, more and more CEOs come from accounting backgrounds. They are a different breed of animal and do not have any form of sympathy, understanding, or forgiveness, as these words do not exist in their limited vocabularies.

Ask not what you can do for your employer. Ask what your employer can do for you (but don't let them know!). I do wish everyone at J&L the very best for the future. From what I hear, they are now turning the corner to becoming the force that they once were in their industry. I hope their future is full of success.

Twenty Three
The Recognition

Remember the Bay City Rollers? Well, I don't have a story about them, but I do have one about Bay City, Michigan. The band apparently chose their name by sticking a pin into a map of U.S., but Bay City is even more famous for its yacht races. This annual event is one of the biggest parties I've ever been to, lasting for four days, and involving boats and crews from all over the U.S. plus quite a number of foreign entries from around the world.

I did this event for four consecutive years before moving to Florida, and the stories of the people are endless. I had an acquaintance named Paul Thomas, who was a member of the very exclusive Bay City Yacht Club, which was situated right on the point where the Black River joins with the St. Claire River. All the yachts would come in on Wednesday and Thursday, and on Friday night, the eve of the race, there was an invitation-only party for the boat owners, crews, and local dignitaries.

Most of the boats were ocean-going vessels, because the race was from Bay City to Mackinaw Island on Lake Huron, one of the five Great Lakes bordering the U.S. and Canada. For four consecutive years, I talked my way into this invitation-only event. I used Paul Thomas' name and always insisted that he'd instructed me to meet him at the side-gate entrance but that I'd missed him.

The place was jam-packed with all these beautiful jet-setting people, and I'd be damned if anybody was going to stand between me and these Ray Milland-esque parties! After causing quite a stir and, at the same time, virtually blocking the gate, thereby making it extremely difficult for anyone else to get in or out, they would reluctantly let me in.

One of the largest yachts was moored right next to the party, and standing there looking up at its fifty-foot masts, I saw it was flying the Welsh flag. The boat, *The Griffin*, was owned by a millionaire from Detroit named Griffin and was the pride of the fleet.

After engaging this gentleman in conversation, I was invited aboard where we drank champagne and watched the sun rise while at the same time listening to a Scottish piper saluting the dawn. Believe me, it doesn't get any better than that!

Driving back down from Port Huron to Detroit the next afternoon, I heard on my car radio an announcement that the city of Pontiac was having a music festival that very day. The star attraction was Brian Setzer (of the Stray Cats fame) and his swing band. I peeled off the expressway and headed over to Pontiac. The event was taking place on the top level of a parking structure right in the downtown section. The music could be heard at street level without actually seeing the bands.

After three straight days of partying, I didn't even have enough money for the entrance fee. I was sitting on a wall listening to the music when up came a young couple who proceeded to jitterbug on the sidewalk right next to me. After about thirty minutes of practice dancing, they asked if I was going to the festival, and when I told them of my predicament, they promptly produced free passes and gave them to me. Up to the top level we all went, and I was amazed to see all these young people dressed in 1950s garb and jitterbugging to beat the band. Brian Setzer is solely responsible for the resurgence of what I used to call "jiving."

My wife is ever amazed at the number of times that I will meet people and can pin-point, very closely, where they come from in Britain just by listening to them speak for a few minutes. This probably comes from the fact that my last job in the United Kingdom took me all over the country.

Like the time we walked into one of our local island bars and ended up discovering that the guy next to me had played rugby against me over thirty years ago. Just by listening to him, it set off a conversation which finally led to the fact that he, Neville Morrall, played at center for Old Parkonians of Birkenhead at the very same time that I was playing center for Port Sunlight. Old Parks was one of our keenest rivals, and the matches we played against each other were no place for the "faint of heart." Blood flowed freely, and it was nothing for at least one player to be banished from the field of play for some dastardly deed.

I vividly remember their iron man, Dave Smith, for the ferocity of his bone-crunching tackles. It was nothing for him to lay an opposing player out cold. On another occasion Sharon and I were sitting at the Beach Front Café when two couples from England sat at the next table to us. I leaned toward Sharon and said one word, Scousers (people from Merseyside). I struck up a conversation with them only to find out that one couple had lived at 2 Chesterfield Avenue, Eastham, whereas my best friend on Merseyside, Pete Metcalfe, lived at 4 Chesterfield Avenue, Eastham, right next door.

This couple had now moved to another address, but I told them that on one of my visits I had to go through their backyard and had to climb over their fence to get into Pete's backyard as I had been locked out of the house, but knew the back door to be unlocked. The Scouser said that he had seen some mysterious footprints in his backyard and had reported the incident to the police as being a possible intruder. Mysterysolved. I was invited to visit Key West for my first experience with their Fantasy Fest, which is on a par with Mardi Gras in New Orleans, making it probably the second- best party in America. I toured all the local watering holes, but found to my liking Captain Tony's just off Duval Street. Captain Tony drank in the company of Earnest Hemingway in his heyday and told me that Hemingway was a cheap drunk. (If you really want to know the truth, ask an old person.) I told Captain Tony that I had previously met him at the memorial service for a well-known Detroit News columnist named Shelby Strothers.

Each famous person that patronizes Captain Tony's Bar is honored by having his name embossed on a bar stool so people can tell that celebrities such as Bob Dylan and Jimmy Buffet have been customers. I looked around the bar and found Shelby's stool and sitting on it, I ordered up a cocktail that he would've been proud of. I got on the phone and called Scott Martelle in California and told him where I was and what I was doing. Scott had introduced me to Shelby several years previously and had always told me that if I found myself in Key West that I should honor Shelby by visiting Captain Tony's, sitting on his personalized stool, and having a drink to his memory. Of all the things that I did while in Key West, I will cherish this the most.

I will ever remember Shelby's relating to me his hilarious story of a visit he made to a pub in London, England which was predominantly patronized by dwarfs and midgets. This absolutely classic tale and others can be found in his book entitled *Saddlebags*.

Twenty Four
The Reward

So here I am living in paradise surrounded by rich, beautiful people who seek excitement and relief from their overpopulated cities like New York, Boston, Chicago, Detroit, Cleveland, and Pittsburgh.

Do I regret any of my past? Not one bit. Look at all the places I've been, all the people I've met, and all the wonderful friends I've made. Have I upset people along the way? Some, but none that mattered to me, otherwise I would have gone out of my way to apologize to them.

My health is good and nothing bothers me. Almost everyone I meet is happy because they either live on this beautiful island full time, or they have enough money to be able to visit here several times during the year. The crime rate here is minor compared with most places in the world. There are plenty of wonderful restaurants, and, of course, ocean fish is one of the staples. Fish like grouper, yellow fin tuna, mahi-mahi, sea bass, snapper, and tilapia are all plentiful. I am surrounded by nature and often encounter dolphin, flamingos, bald eagles, ospreys, stingrays, pelicans, and parrots. I wake up almost every day to sunshine, and the plant life is outstanding. My yard (garden) has fir trees, palm trees, hibiscus, ferns, ivy, yuccas, and cactus. I can walk the beach and find dozens of different seashells and sharks' teeth. Because of the climate, it costs very little to survive here, clothing being particularly inexpensive. I mainly wear shorts, a short-sleeved buttoned shirt, and sandals. Beer is cheap, and the living is easy.

I finished playing soccer about a year after I arrived here, at the age of sixty-one. I wasn't playing for an organized team, but turned up at a park and played pickup games with predominately Mexican players. The last game I played, I scored what was probably one of the best goals I have ever scored. I was playing on the left wing, because anyone who knows me well will tell you that I'm a left footer. A teammate on the opposite side of the field kicked the ball across the field from the half-way line. The center forward, a short Mexican boy, was going for the ball, but I could see that it was coming at such a speed that it was going to go over his head and was heading in my direction. I ran to it and met it perfectly. The ball flew off my head with such velocity that it was in the back of the net before the goalkeeper moved.

Thinking back to my last game of rugby at the age of thirty-six and how I scored a try then, I decided to end my playing days right there. Two years later, I arranged for my old Michigan team, the Canton Celtics, to come down to Florida and play against the Sarasota Football Club. They played two games, the second being a little more casual, and for the last fifteen minutes I went in as a substitute.

The score was tied at four apiece, and Gary Bell came over to me and said, "Lyn, you're going to score the winner." A few minutes later, Gary latched onto a through ball and was closing in on a goal. Knowing exactly what he would do, I took off running. The keeper came out to narrow the angle. Gary waited until he was two yards from him and pushed the ball to his right and put me through on an open goal. Enough said?

I walked into the Drift Inn, a small bar in the small town where I live. It's nothing pretentious, just a shot-and-beer bar with a good jukebox. I ordered a beer, and as I looked down the bar, I saw one of my all-time idols.

"You look an awful lot like Willie John McBride," I said to the guy.

"Oh, really, then where do I come from?" he replied.

"Ballymena," I replied.

"What religion am I?" was his next question.

To which I retorted, "I never discuss religion in a bar, Willie."

At this he rose from his stool, came around the bar, and putting his shovel-sized hand on my shoulder said, "You'll be having a drink with me," and I was in no position to say no.

This man had captained probably the finest combined British and Irish rugby team to leave our shores. They went to South Africa and New Zealand and took everything before them. We swapped stories of Ray Prosser, "Broon" from Troon, JPR, and Willie Duggan. It was a most magical moment, and I couldn't believe that of all the places that Willie John had traveled to in his illustrious career, I should bump into him on Anna Maria Island. It just goes to show that, if you want to meet fame, you have to go where fame is. This incident rivaled my meeting George Best twenty-odd years earlier.

Yet another major rugby incident occurred when, about a year later my wife and I walked into the same Drift Inn on Bridge Street in my home town in Bradenton Beach. I spotted two couples seated at a table, and I asked the barmaid, Doreen, if they were Brits, to which she replied that they were. Eventually, as almost always happens in a small bar, we ended up having a conversation with them. I was amazed to find out that one of the men was no less than Gary Stevens, an ex-Rugby League scrum-half, who had represented Great Britain. He had played for his hometown of Castleford and had a spell with Wigan before winning the British Challenge Cup with Halifax. He was invited to play in Australia for a team named Manly, near Sydney, and ended up winning the

Australian Rugby League Championship with them and was awarded the trophy for "Man of the Match," or MVP as we say in America.

This unassuming man, in his playing days, had been as tough as nails and was tricky and skillful in every facet of the game he played. We rounded off the night with everyone coming back to our house for a few nightcaps and to hear more of Gary's incredible rugby stories. Once again the Island of Anna Maria had lured yet another sportsman of great celebrity.

Maybe inspired by these monumental meetings, at aged sixty-three I decided to get involved with rugby again. The Sarasota Red Tide Rugby Club needed some help, as their coach had just hurriedly departed and left them hanging. I am not exactly a coach, more like an advisor of the game, particularly for the backs. I traveled with them to their last away game of the spring season. We had exactly fifteen players and me. We were playing Orlando Iron Horse, and five minutes into the game our young winger, playing his first game, broke a bone in his foot and had to limp off. Our captain, Ollie McConnell, asked me if I could go out on the right wing and generally make a nuisance of myself. At sixty-three and twenty-seven years after my last game, I went on to the pitch and played out the remaining seventy-five minutes with brittle bones and no insurance. I must have been crazy, but I felt all that old piss and vinegar running through my veins again——that great feeling of putting your jersey over your head and running onto the field.

We ended up losing seventeen points to twelve, and we crossed their line twice in the closing minutes but just could not ground the ball in spite of the valiant efforts of Joe O'Neil.

No, unlike some of my other crowning sporting moments, I did not score or even look like scoring a try. On the other hand, none of their three tries were scored on my side of the park.

When the game ended, the whole opposing team shook my hand and thanked me saying that this was the type of occasion that makes the game of rugby what it is. In what other sport could you see such heroics or — — according to my wife — — such stupidity? The Red Tide has had its numbers diminished for this fall season, but a quick phone call back to Wales, and coach David Manley is sending me three players from the University of Wales, Cardiff (UWIC).

Here we go again! Where will it all end?

Twenty Five
Near Misses (UK)

If a cat has nine lives, then I should have been a cat because, in my lifetime, I have had eight near misses with death. I was almost killed twice while living in South Wales, even though each event happened elsewhere. I was almost killed twice while living on Merseyside (England) and almost killed a further four times while living in the U.S. Four of these incidents were automobile-related, two were airplane-related, one was water-related, and the other was a (legal) drug-related accident. As my daughter, Louise, once told me, I have only one more near miss left, and that might then be all she wrote for me!

I have already mentioned two of the above incidents: one when I was miss-prescribed some tablets containing an over-amount of Atropine, which almost completely paralyzed me. The second occurred when I spun my car off the road, one dark and icy morning on my way to Frankenmuth, Michigan, and ended up in a ditch. On both occasions, Lady Luck played her hand, and I survived those potentially fatal incidents without even a scratch.

The trouble with being a wanderer like me is that so many other peoples' mistakes might fall at your doorstep. The crisscrossing of so many peoples' lives cause anover-

111

abundance of opportunities for something to go wrong. Each day on the roads, in the air, and even at sea, there are so many times that lives are lost or saved by a matter of inches or seconds. Everyone has their mind set on what they have to do that day or where they have to go to such an extent that their bodies and minds are not always in sync with what's going on around them, and this can sometimes prove fatal.

Take the time I went to Bristol (England) for the weekend with my friend, Russell Ivory. At seventeen, I was game for anything that would add a little excitement to my Life, and a couple of days out of the Valleys was right up my street.

Russell and I were waiting to cross the road at a very busy intersection, and on this particular Saturday the traffic lights seemed to take forever. So the two of us, being impetuous, set off across the road through the rows of cars. The first two lanes of traffic were at a standstill and posed no problems.

Seeing that the lanes on the other side of the road were clear, I started to run across. What I had failed to notice was that there were actually three lanes of traffic on our side of the road, the third lane being the left-turn lane. As I rushed out into this third lane, there appeared from nowhere a low, two-seater sports car doing around fifty mph, trying to make the lights before they turned red again. I did not see this car as I began to race across the lane. Lucky for me, my pal Russell did see it, and grabbing the collar of my jacket, he yanked me back out of harm's way. Had he not done this, there might have been an extremely bad collision. In cases of automobile versus pedestrian, inevitably the pedestrian comes off second best. It is thanks to Russell Ivory that I am able to relate this story today.

My next near miss was on a trip down to the south of Spain, when I was eighteen. About ten of the Girling apprentices went on a two-week continental trip arranged by Mr. Ivory, Russell's father, who was the apprentices' supervisor. After the better part of three days, spent crammed in a hot, sticky van, we finally reached our destination late in the day. We literally only had time to pitch our tents and roll into our sleeping bags before nightfall.

The next day, we arose bright and early, andafter a quick bite to eat, we all rushed into the Mediterranean Sea for a dip. What our untrained eyes failed to notice was that there was a heavy swell and a vicious undercurrent, or riptide, as they say in U.S.

Weighing just 120 pounds, I was knocked about by the heavy waves, and, time and time again, the sheer weight of the water drove me down to the sandy bottom. After what seemed a lifetime, I literally clawed my way along the sea bottom before dragging myself, totally exhausted, back onto the beach. Although they were only a few yards away from me, my friends had no idea that I was almost drowning and that, if I'd not stayed under the water, I would have been dragged out to sea.

Living now in Florida, I am now very aware of when not to go into the sea. Almost every year, around forty people are lost here due to the vicious riptides.

The Atropine Experience, as I like to call it, happened in Bromborough (England) as did another near fatal incident. I was on New Chester Road one morning around 6:45 a.m. on my way to Girling Ltd. for the 7:00 a.m. shift. It was very dark, extremely wet, and my vehicle was positioned at the center of the road, ready for a right turn the minute the on-coming traffic had passed.

Seeing that the road was now clear, I had just begun my turn when I fortuitously happened to glance in my side mirror, which was mounted on the front driver's side of the hood. From out of nowhere, a huge semi truck was overtaking me on the wrong side of the road. I braked quickly, and the sheer wind of the passing juggernaut moved my car about two feet sideways. Because the driver never hit his brakes or gave me any warning of his approach, I have assumed he had either fallen asleep or had some medical condition. If I had swung across into his path, I would have taken the full impact of the collision on the driver's side. At the speed he was going, around seventy mph, there would have been no way I could have survived.

I was so shaken up by this incident that my manager, Clive Walker, sent me home for the rest of the day.

I heard later that evening on the news that two people had been killed in a bad road accident on New Chester Road. I can only speculate that the same semi truck was involved.

There but for the grace of God go I!

Twenty Six
Near Misses (US)

I have already mentioned one of these near misses, where I spun my car off an icy road early one winter's morning on my way to Frankenmuth, Michigan. There were three other occasions when I came extremely close to meeting my Maker. Two of these occurred during air flights, and the third was another driving incident.

I was on a business trip to Houston, Texas, and on arriving at the airport for the return flight, I was told that I could not fly to Detroit via Dallas because there were horrendous thunderstorms in that region; all flights had been either canceled or delayed. I was given an alternative: fly to Detroit via Washington, D.C. I was in a hurry, so I agreed to the flight change. It wasn't until I was actually on the plane that I found out that our destination was not Dulles International Airport, but Washington National Airport, in downtown Washington. This didn't bother me too much — — until we began descending into Washington. In fact, we were flying up the Potomac River with buildings on either side of us that were higher than the plane was. I remember seeing people sitting at their desks, going about their daily activities, and I wondered if they could see me as clearly as I could see them.

We finally landed, and after about an hour the Detroit

flight began boarding. I shuffled on along with the other cold, tired, and fed-up passengers.

Now at this time of year, Washington was in the middle of a blizzard, which had battered the city for the past four days. Consequently, after boarding the plane and sitting on the runway for about thirty minutes, the plane taxied over to a deicing bay for the wings to be sprayed. This was repeated, some twenty minutes later, and finally the airline felt confident enough to allow us to depart.

We began to taxi down the runway at breakneck speed, with all engines screaming. Then, with a jolt, we lunged upward into the night sky. The plane was heavily weighted with ice, and we cleared a bridge on which the traffic was lined up bumper to bumper by no more by twenty feet. It was pitch black, and as we approached and then passed over one particular car, I could see the driver's eyes grow as large as an owl's as we hurtled past him. Only the passengers seated at the windows knew how near we came to hitting that bridge.

Just two days later, a flight did hit that very same bridge and ended up in the Potomac River. As I watched the rescue operation on TV, a cold chill ran up my spine, just as if someone had walked over my grave. Some twenty-odd people died in the tragedy. Needless to say, I never took a flight through that airport again!

My second air incident happened on a little commuter plane (a crop sprayer) with only myself, the pilot, and one other passenger on board. I was on a business trip to Des Moines, Iowa, and decided to visit a potential customer in a little town called Spencer, up near the South Dakota border. We took off on a beautifully clear, sunny summer's day, with just a few puffy white clouds floating by. The flight was, at first, uneventful, and I was talking to the other passenger, an executive from Eaton Corporation, the customer I was due to visit.

At this stage, the pilot must have had the plane on autopilot because he was reading a book or manual or something. I happened to glance out of the window, and I saw, off in the distance, a small dot — —another plane— —coming toward us from the northeast. At first, I thought nothing of it. It was a clear day, and both planes could surely see each other from miles away. A few minutes passed, and on glancing out of the window again, I could see that the dot was now a definite object rapidly closing in on us and on what seemed to be a collision course. I was only about six feet from the pilot, so I leaned forward and asked him if he was aware that we were not alone in the friendly skies.

He glanced out of his window; and with about ten expletives all rolled into one, grabbed the controls and did one of those Red-Baron maneuvers. The planes passed each other by about two hundred yards, the other plane passing under us as we did some fancy aerobatics. I believe that a near miss, in flying terms, is anything under one half of a mile. If this is the case, then I can truthfully say that I've seen the Pearly Gates half open and heard St. Peter calling my name!

When we landed, the pilot was groveling with apologies. I wish now that I'd asked him what was so bloody interesting in that damn book!

The last of my eight near misses happened when I was driving south down I-275, around the Livonia/Canton area of Michigan, on a normal afternoon run between customer calls. I had just entered the expressway and had moved from the slow lane to the middle lane. I was using all my mirrors because I was getting ready to move over into the fast lane and needed to know exactly where all the vehicles around me were located. All of a sudden, there was this god-awful crash in front of me, and a huge semi tractor-trailer jackknifed across all the lanes. If I'd carried straight on in the lane I was in, I would have hit the trailer dead center, and the collision would have taken the top of my car clean off.

In a split-second, I realized that the vehicle driving alongside of me, in the fast lane, had hit the brakes and almost stood on end. This opened up the fast lane and gave me about twenty to thirty yards before I'd reach the semi, so I braked once and swung my car into the now-empty fast lane. The semi had blocked all three lanes, but I passed it on the hard shoulder outside the fast lane, missing it with about a foot to spare!

The semi had hit, head-on, a car driven by an eighty-year-old woman, who'd somehow gotten onto the southbound lane and was heading north. The semi driver could do nothing to avoid her, and I believe she died on impact. I was so shaken up that I phoned my boss, told him the details, and told him I was finishing work for the day. He had some difficulty in grasping the situation until he saw it on the television evening news later that night. Several drivers were also injured to a lesser degree in the aftermath of the crash. Once again, I had cheated death and thwarted the Grim Reaper. I'd also used up the eighth of my nine lives.

Apart from the first two, which occurred when I was a teenager, all the others have been work-related incidents. Going to work, on business, while traveling on company visits, etc. I have now decided that, when the Number 9 comes around, I will be somewhere I want to be, doing something for me and my family — —something that I myself have chosen to do. Never again will I put my life in jeopardy for some thankless company who'd forget me one year later. They can kiss my grits!

Twenty Seven
The Melting Pot

I now live about five miles away from one of the largest and best organized sports complexes in the U.S. The Bollettieri Sports Academy began as a tennis-only facility and can boast having tutored such players as Pete Sampras, Andre Agassi, and many, many other famous international stars. It is known all over the world and attracts budding stars from Russia, Germany, France, etc., plus a number of South American countries.

Bollettieri is known the world over as being one of the greatest sports motivators, and his pupils go on to win many internationally known tournaments. Earlier this year the ladies title at Wimbledon was won by another Bollettieri trainee tennis protégé, Maria Sharapova. More recently, the academy has been expanded to offer training and tutoring in the sports of golf and football (soccer). It has now become the home of the U.S. under-17 soccer team.

In Florida they can play all year round, and this goes for tennis and golf too. The players live at the academy all year round and have their schooling there, in-house, as well.

The other day, I was having a cup of coffee at the famous Jackie's Paradise Bagel Café when in walked two young men who, judging by the advertisement on their tee shirts, were on the training staff of the Bollettieri Soccer Academy. I struck up a conversation with them, and they told me that on the upcoming weekend there was to be a huge soccer tournament with teams coming in from all over the U.S. To put the icing on the cake, the Brazil under-17 national team would also be there to play against their American counterparts.

Since I am now a man of leisure, I decided that this would be a great way to spend four days of high-class sporting entertainment. I arrived at the complex early on Friday morning, and after collecting a schedule, I wandered around the various fields, weighing up the abundance of talent. I cast my mind back to 1976, when I had first come to America and how far behind we were compared to the rest of the world. Not anymore! The standard of play from these young men was nothing short of excellent. I have to warn the rest of the world that, in the next twenty years, you will see the U.S. reach the absolute top level of competition. There's already a sixteen-year-old player named Freddie Adu who's making scouts from the larger European clubs monitor his every move. With talent like him coming through, an extra dimension will be added to the world soccer family.

Remember, the U.S. has nationals from around the world, and it is still the biggest melting pot of foreign-born people. You will see Mexicans, Italians, Germans, Poles, British, Irish, and many other names on the American team roster in years to come. All it takes now is four years of residency.

The football (soccer) structure is different here in America from most other countries in the world. Players are monitored from an early age, and their progress from being a high school player can be noted by local and national colleges and universities that give out scholarships to encourage those players to join their sports programs.

Now a scholarship means free, or partly free, tuition for those with talent enough to make the grade. Therefore, this soccer tournament had attracted the coaches from just about every leading college and university in the U.S. Each coach had his own special shopping list, and with every player on each team listed in the program, it was easy for them to pick out and watch how these players performed. All these players, being one year away from finishing high school, were ripe for the picking. With just one year left before selecting which college or university they would go to, an offer of a scholarship would greatly influence the educational direction that they would choose.

By the same token, the players also know which college or university has the best program. Therefore, this under-17 tournament was one big talent-spotting opportunity, and both players and coaches were there to do some horse trading.

With all this in mind, as a soccer purist and for no other reason, I was also wandering around watching the coaches clucking around like so many broody hens tending their chicks. For some reason, a game between a Boston-area team and an Arizona team caught my attention, so I wandered over to the designated field about thirty minutes before kickoff to watch the teams warm up. I was standing on the touchline and struck up a conversation with a man who happened to be the team manager of the Boston outfit. While we were talking, I heard their coach on the field snapping out instructions in a distinctly North English accent. The coach, in a blue tracksuit, sunglasses, and wearing long, shoulder-length hair, seemed somewhat familiar.

I asked the manager who the coach was, and with a wry smile he told me that it was ex-Ipswich, Arsenal, and England center forward, Paul Mariner. While the team trainer began to put the players through some stretching exercises, Paul came over to the sideline where I was standing. Right off the bat I asked him if he had been on Bobby Robson's team that had won the 1980-81 F.A. Cup Final. This brought a smile to his face, and in no time we were deep in conversation about football. I told him of my association with two other players from that great team, Alan Brazil and Roger Osbourne, while they had been with the Detroit Express, and this seemed to relax him even more.

The game was now ready to kick off, so we broke off our conversation, but he invited me to stick around, watch his team play, and said we could continue our chat later.

There were two other men who seemed to be involved in the Boston team's organization. The one turned out to be John Kerr, who was the first American to be signed to a professional soccer contract in England. This was with Portsmouth,where he had played for many years. He was now head coach of Harvard University in Massachusetts. His father, John senior, was also a well-known player in the Scottish League and acted as an advisor for his son.

The second man, who was a long-time friend of Paul Mariner and another soccer nut, was a guy called David Colwell. If anyone knows their music, they'll recognize him as being a member of the band Bad Company. So, here again, my sports and music interests had come together.

I guess being British means that this is not such a far stretch of the imagination. Blue-collar kids in Britain really only have two interests outside of work, those being sports and music, and it's obvious that they will merge sooner or later. Such musicians as Elton John, Rod Stewart, and more recently, Robbie Williams, all have a love for soccer and quite often show it by getting involved in the sport.

As Rod would say, "You're Celtic, United/You're the best thing I've ever seen."

I am so proud to have met so many celebrities from each of these genres.

Twenty Eight
Full Circle

I've told you already about how I met John Lennon and Paul McCartney back in 1964. Two years ago, on one of my many trips back to the old country, I took my wife, Sharon, on a tour of Liverpool— —not an official one, but one conducted solely by me. We caught the ferry over from Birkenhead Woodside Terminal, and after a brief jaunt, with Gerry and the Pacemakers singing "Ferry Cross the Mersey," we arrived at Liverpool Pier Head. From there, we walked up to Matthews Street, the site of the original Cavern Club, which is now a kind of museum dedicated to the Beatles— —souvenirs and memorabilia, etc. We saw the life-size, bronze statues of the Fab Four, which at that time, was festooned with floral tributes to Linda (Eastman) McCartney, who had recently and tragically passed away.

Sharon sat on a bench next to a bronzed statue of "Eleanor Rigby" as she (fictitiously) fed the pigeons. We still have the photograph to this day, and I've enshrined it next to my photo of me and a life-size, bronze statue of John Lennon leaning in a doorway.

While eating a pork pie at the old Abbey Road Pub, we saw a copy of all four Beatles' birth certificates and were entertained by an entrepreneur trying to sell me some socks out of a suitcase. Shades of "Del Boy." Luverly Jubberly!

This is all part of Liverpool's rich tapestry— —even the sock man. Afterward I showed Sharon the Green Door, the Pink Parrot (now a derelict building), and the Jacaranda Bar.

Many people think that the Beatles started their careers at the Cavern Club. Long before Ringo replaced Pete Best as their drummer, the group was playing at the Jacaranda Bar. In their very early days, Stuart Sutcliffe's parents, particularly his mother, ran the Jacaranda Bar, so the Beatles were allowed to play in the small, downstairs room. It had a small bar, a small stage, a small dance floor, and a small alcove with one booth-style table and bench seats. It is said that the Beatles composed a lot of their earlier hits while sitting in that little alcove, so Sharon, being Sharon, had to slide all along each of the bench seats, just to ensure she had all the seating options covered. The Jacaranda Bar has some of the absolutely best black-and-white, early photographs of the original Fab Five.

On another Liverpool visit, Sharon and I were accompanied by my daughter, Louise, and her son, Jack (my grandson). This time, we took a good look around the refurbished Albert Dock. We then decided to visit the Beatles Experience and were a little disappointed to discover that all cameras and video-recorders had to be left at the door. Earlier, and on a similar UK visit, we'd visited the Blacksmith's Museum at Gretna Green, Scotland, close to the Scottish border with England. We'd not noticed the no-cameras sign and had walked through snapping just about everything there was to see! It wasn't until we'd left the museum that we noticed the sign! However, and unlike our Scottish hosts, the Scousers patted us down and confiscated all offending items.

We had a good look around, and as we exited and collected our cameras, we noticed a crowd of people gathering at the rear of a truck marked Sotheby's. We wandered over, and there on the tail-lift of the truck, much to our astonishment, was John Lennon's old upright piano! John had only owned two pianos in his lifetime. One was an all-white Steinway grand piano, which was located at his Dakota Apartments' home in New York. The other was this same upright. This one had been donated for viewing at the Beatles Experience in Liverpool. It was now being transported to London to be auctioned off to the highest bidder (another Yoko-ism).

This old, simple, well-worn upright piano was the one on which he'd composed and written the lyrics for the number-one voted record of all times, "Imagine." To me, this was a piece of music history, and can you believe my luck to be there at that very spot and at the very moment the piano had been released from its no-camera tomb? While several reporters from various TV channels took turns in relating the piano's remarkable story, I was hopping all over the place, snapping away from every conceivable angle.

The bottom line of this story is that George Michael bought the piano for £2 million and then gave it back to the Beatles Experience for future fans to see. Unlike me, however, they will certainly never be able to photograph it!

Another full-circle story is one where I was on a business trip to Sweden in 1969. I was in the small town of Sandviken and was staying at the local hotel/bar/restaurant. I was in the habit of taking a few drinks before dinner, and each time I went into the bar, everybody treated me like a long-lost brother. I was certainly amazed by their friendliness and generosity. Some nights the other customers would not let me pay for a drink, and the other guys with me on the business training course began asking me what the hell was going on? I didn't know, and in my defense, I could only suggest that they seemed to like me for some inexplicable reason. I was certainly not going to spoil a good thing by asking them why.

By the end of my two-week stay, even I had become curious and asked the bartender what was going on. He smiled and said that all these people thought I was a famous Swedish ice hockey player. The bartender knew I wasn't, but he kept this to himself. For that, I gave him a generous tip.

Just about a year ago, in 2003, I was coaching a rugby team called the Sarasota Red Tide, in Florida (U.S.). One of the players was a Scottish lad named Ewan Robertson, who worked for a Swedish company that installed yacht decks made from teakwood. We had several parties at his home, and often he would invite some of his work colleagues along too. Some of these guys were from Sweden.

One night, after a particularly arduous drinking session, I related the previously mentioned Sandviken incident.

At the end of my tale, the whole Swedish contingent in the room yelled in unison, "Hardy Nilsson! You look like Hardy Nilsson!"

Apparently, Hardy Nilsson was a superstar of the Swedish National ice hockey team, and at the end of his illustrious playing career, he had become equally famous as the national team's coach for many years. This man was huge, revered all around the world, and adored and idolized throughout his native Scandinavia!

If I'd only known the magnitude of my "doppelganger," I think I could have milked it for a few more free drinks. Since obtaining this information, I can now, in my best Swedish accent, declare, "I'm Hardy Nilsson — — the schnapps are on me!"

Twenty Nine
The Payoff

Just recently on a month's visit to England and Wales, I found myself in Cardiff for the Wales vs. Scotland rugby international match. Once again my old friend Pete Morrell had gotten my wife and me tickets to the game plus lunch at the Hilton Hotel before the game and an invitation to the post-game party— —all the auspices of that fine organization, the Newport Saracen's RUFC, to whom I am forever indebted. Everything was magnificent: the food, the comradeship, the organization— —all top class.

After lunch we strolled across to the stadium, found our seats, and settled in for a fine afternoon's rugby. From the first scrum on the Welsh twenty-two meter line, Wales ran the ball in brilliant fashion and scored a try (touchdown), and I knew from that point onward that Wales would win that day. They did with a score of twenty-three points to ten in their favor.

On the way back to the Hilton, we stopped at some of Cardiff's finest watering holes including The Rummer, the Goat Major, and Dempsey's Irish Bar. Back at the Hilton Arthur Young was emceeing the party in his own inimitable style, and everyone was in good humor.

We met up with Lyndsey Lewis and his wife, Annette,

and Jeff and Sandra Cranton. Now Jeff in his rugby-playing days had won the Welsh unofficial championship (with Pontypool) and the Welsh Cup (with Newport) in consecutive years in the mid 1970s. He was jokingly known as Stuecker, after the World War II German fighter plane, since an incident where he laid out an opposing player after dropping on him from an amazingly high altitude.

Anyway, we were all standing at the bar listening to the usual rugby banter, when Pete Morrell told me that he had just seen several of that days' Welsh team in the gents' toilet. With pen and paper in hand, I set off for the same location, but when I arrived the amenities were completely empty. I came back to the hallway and realized there was another doorway leading to another function room, and sure enough I opened that door, and there they all were.

At the time I was wearing casual street clothes, and this was a black-tie affair. This reception was for players, team officials, and dignitaries only. Without hesitation I strode into the room and made straight for Colin Charvis (the Welsh captain) and asked for his autograph, which he very graciously gave. I suddenly realized that, unlike almost everyone else at the reception, Colin was wearing a maroon bowtie, and then the penny dropped. I glanced around the room and could immediately pick out all of the players from their black-tie counterparts. It didn't take me very long to locate most of the players, and even not dressed in proper attire, not one of them turned me down or even asked who I was or why I was there.

At this time my wife, having been stopped at the front door, had found the back entrance and had now joined me among this wealth of dignitaries. As Sean Williams, Iestyn Harris, and Ceri Sweeney were signing for me, I told them that as a fan of Welsh rugby I was not only impressed by the win, but by the manner in which it had been accomplished. I told them that they were beginning to remind me of the great 1970s Welsh teams. This brought broad grins from these young men, and they shook my handin appreciation.

Out of the twenty-two squad players on the team sheet that day, I managed to speak to and get autographs from seventeen.

At this point, we were approached by a high-ranking dignitary, and we were politely asked to leave, which we did without any objections or hesitation.

On returning to our function room, we told our companions of our unscheduled visit. Some of them indicated that they too would like to attempt such a sneak attack. However, the hotel security had now realized their mistake by not having anyone at the rear door, and they had corrected the oversight.

Once again the Clarke luck had prevailed. Or was it more the case that acting on experience and instinct, I had pulled off yet another *coupe de gras* of the most audacious kind. Whichever is the reason, it does not detract from the fact that I'm still going to famous occasions and meeting famous people.

In all the years of these momentous events, I have never had any famous person snub or refuse to talk to me. So long as I behave humble and polite, I know that I will be received well. Incidentally, since meeting Iestyn Harris, he has returned to his rugby league roots. He will be a big loss to the Welsh rugby union scene, but I wish him and his new team, the Bradford Bulls, all the best for their upcoming season.

Another rugby story, which took an unexpected turn, happened toward the end of the three-month visit to my home, by the three University of Wales, Cardiff (U.W.I.C) rugby players. Harry Trelawney, Gareth Richards, and Ross Gilling came to Florida to play rugby for me. They were a lot of fun. They worked hard, and they played even harder, eventually winning the Florida Rugby Cup while guesting for the St. Petersburg Pelicans.

Before leaving, one of them, Ross, met an absolutely charming young American lady, Sarah, who has now changed her name from Hunter to Gilling. I'm so happy for them both and was proud to attend their wedding in Cocoa Beach. Ross' new father-in-law, Mike Hunter, was a baseball player on the books with the New York Yankees. I guess to my list of jobs, you can now add matchmaker.

I could not close my thoughts on rugby without remembering some of the absolute best players that I have been lucky enough to have played with or against in my heyday. I will list the teams that they were playing for when I met them on the rugby field:

(15) Sam Doble - fullback (St.Paul's, Cheltenham and England)
(14) Mike Sleman - wing (Liverpool and England)
(13) Malcolm Price - center (Abersychan Tech and Wales)
(12) Tom Brophy - center (Liverpool and England)
(11) Laurie Daniels - wing (Twmpath School and Wales)
(10) David Watkins - out half (Cwmcelyn Youth and Wales)
(9) Steve Smith – scrum half (Old Wirralians and England)
(1) Graham Price - prop (Alsager College and Wales)
(2) Graham Bevan - hooker (Girling Apprentices and Monmouthshire)
(3) Norman Colclough - prop (Port Sunlight and Cheshire)
(4) Bill Morris - lock (Wrexham and Wales)
(5) Eric Phillips - lock (Girling Apprentices and Monmouthshire)
(6) Des Seabrooke - wing forward (Orrell and Lancashire)
(8) John Stanley - loose forward (Pontypool United and Monmouthshire)
(7) John White - wing forward (St.Pauls Cheltenham and England)

Also very worthy of mention are:
(a) Paul Watts - wing forward (Girling Apprentices and Monmouthshire)

(b)   Brian Redwood - scrum half (St.Pauls Cheltenham
and   England)
(c)   Graham Tovey - center (Girling RUFC and
       Monmouthshire)
(d)   Peter Ashcroft - out half (Port Sunlight and Cheshire)
(e)   Ray Cheyne - fullback (Girling RUFC and
       Monmouthshire)
(f)   Roy Laidlaw - center (Jed Forrest and St. Boswell's
       Scotland)
(g)   John Harris - lock (Girling Apprentices and Ponypool)
(h)   Bobby Lewis - fullback (Port Sunlight and Cheshire)
(i)   Graham Bishop - lock (St. James Youth and
       Monmouthshire)
(j)   Dennie Bonner - center (Port Sunlight and Cheshire)
(k)   Mike Nicholas - loose forward (Briton Ferry and
       Wales Rugby League)
(l)   Bill Capener - fullback (Port Sunlight and Cheshire)
(m)   Jim Hartey - center (Old Anselmians and Cheshire)

Mike Nicholas would have been included in my All-Star XV if it were not for the fact that he represented Wales in rugby league instead of rugby union. Poor Sam Doble died of cancer at the height of his rugby career. He could kick a rugby ball farther than anyone else that I have ever known.

Thirty
The Revival

    Since moving from the state of Michigan, on the Canadian border, to the Sunshine State of Florida, I have become quite fascinated with the southern rock music scene. Two of the best bands of this genre and both most famous way before I moved to Dixie were the Lynyrd Skynyrd Band and the Allman Brothers. By the time I arrived here, some five years ago, both these groups were no longer playing. Down here, however, their music raged on and can be heard on almost any bar jukebox.

    My wife and I used to frequent a great bar/restaurant called Bongo's over by Perico Island. Sadly the bar also became a casualty of some fickle real estate dealings. Lucky for me just before Bongo's went down, they put on a free concert of the Lynyrd Skynyrd Revival Band. The original band was decimated by a plane crash from which only two people survived. They had been flying on a single-engine crop sprayer from one small town to a gig at some equally small town when − −would you believe?− −their plane ran out of fuel. Only Artimus Pyle, the drummer, and one backup singer, a lady, got out alive. This was back in the late '70s, and here we are now in the early twenty-first century, and the Skynyrd sound is back.

The original singer, Ronnie Van Zant, was replaced by his younger cousin Donnie, who looked remarkably like him and even more amazingly sounded almost identical. The new band had the three-guitar sound that they were famous for, which rocks, and the rhythm section that drove the music along. They played just about all of the original classics — — "Three Steps to the Door," "Free Bird," "Saturday Night Special," "What's Your Name (Little Girl)," "Sweet Home Alabama," — — and many others that will always be synonymous with these great southern rock legends.

I recently saw an old black-and-white videotape from a concert in the grounds of some English castle, where they had been one of the opening acts for the Rolling Stones at the height of their popularity. Skynyrd blew them away, and the crowd would not let them off the stage, much to the chagrin of the Stones, whose performance paled into insignificance. That night at Bongo's was the nearest I will ever be to witnessing one of the truly best rock bands to this day.

This past spring, and about a year after the Skynyrd incident, the city of Bradenton was having a street festival with people selling all kinds of different items throughout the day and at night they had live music. The festival lasted for three days and nights, but on the Saturday night the live music was by a band called the Toler Brothers.

Now this is of interest to me because the Toler Brothers (Dangerous Dan (guitar) and Frankie (drums)) had played with the original Allman Brothers' Band and because of that were quite famous down in these parts. I joined the excited crowd and settled in to listen to another part of the South's music history.

Across the crowd, I saw a friend of mine, Mark Kracker, who had been working throughout the weekend with each band, helping with the setup of all the lighting and microphones. He was waving at me frantically and beckoning my wife and me to join him. We pushed our way through the crowd, and linking up with Mark, he escorted us right up to the edge of the stage. He said that he had a surprise for me and told me that another original member of Allman Brothers' Band had turned up unannounced: Dickie Betts.

Now Dickie had been a hard-drinking party animal in the years gone by. He had wrecked his fame and fortune, but now he was back to his absolute best. On taking a short while to warm up his guitar, he jumped right into "Rambling Man," my all-time Allman Brothers favorite. The chills were running up and down my spine, and the hair was upright on my neck.

Once again, as with Skynyrd, I had experienced something that very few people living today have had the good fortune to see in the flesh. There's an old saying down here in Dixie; they say that the South will rise again. Although this will not happen in the same context as the Civil War, as far as music is concerned, they have already risen, what with Bluegrass music from Kentucky, the Virginias, and Tennessee. Country music from Nashville beginnings and the now New Country music with all those amazing artists like Toby Keith, Shania Twain, Clint Black, and Garth Books — — the South is doing just fine. Shania, of course, is Canadian, but her heart is in the southern states of America.

When I was seventeen, I first saw Tom Jones at the Memo Dance Hall at Newbridge and coming from the south — — South Wales, that is — — he is the only star that has come out of Wales that could hold a candle to these massive singer/musicians that America turns out year after year. Most of these megastars even write their own lyrics, which impresses me even more. If you ever go to see Tom Jones in concert, don't forget to wave your Welsh flag; he loves to see that.

Another singer worthy of mention and running in tandem with Tom Jones was a relatively unknown young man named Jerry Dorsey. When I first saw him, he was singing with the Ted Heath Band at a dance in the Girling's company canteen. I was nineteen, and on this particular Saturday night I was jiving with my dance partner Nora Williams (now Blake) when I remarked to her that, not only was this young man an extremely good singer, he was also distinctively handsome. He seemed to fade off into obscurity, and no one knew what happened to him until he popped up again out of the blue with a new name. As Englebert Humperdink, he became as popular in Las Vegas as Tom Jones.

As a notable talent, I would like to mention a unique Florida local boy that I see and talk with virtually every week on Anna Marie Island. His name is Koko Ray, and he has currently the liveliest southern rock band in these parts. The main contributing factor is that Koko himself plays an alto and a tenor saxophone--at the same time--which produces a unique sound. He occasionally--at the same time--smokes a cigarette as well. Amazing!

Another saxophone story happened during my recent visit to Las Vegas. I went there for a week, but Hurricane Jeanne closed down the major southern airports of Atlanta, Dallas, and Tampa, thus extending my visit for another two days. To get back to my home on Anna Maria Island, I had to fly into Ft. Lauderdale and then hire a car to make a four-hour journey via Alligator Alley from the East Coast to the West.

It was right in the middle of Freemont Street in the Old Town section of Las Vegas that I met Carl Ferris— —right at the intersection where the Four Queens Casino, Binnion's Horseshoe Casino, the Golden Nugget Casino, and Sam Boyde's Freemont Casino all converge.

Carl was warming up the considerable crowd that had gathered there to witness the spectacular laser light show, which is staged on Freemont Street nightly. He was knocking out numbers on all three saxophones, the soprano, the alto, and the tenor, and his pure tones mixed with an infectious rhythm had everybody tapping their toes and clapping their hands. Now this cat could play and would, in my humble opinion, overshadow some of the more famous musicians, such as Kenny G, by a long shot.

I was so impressed that I returned to see him a second

time a few nights later. Again, he was playing only his own compositions such as "Feed the Chicken" and the very catchy "On Freemont Street," but this time the crowd appreciating his performance was twice as large and more enthusiastic.

As he took a break, I asked him if I could have a word with him, and being the totally unaffected guy that he is, he agreed. We went and sat at two slot machines just inside a nearby bar, and I told him my story of how I met Stan Getz, which he thoroughly enjoyed, at the end of which I reached into my wallet and took out Stan's autograph and pressed it into the palm of his hand. "Carl, you are the free spirit which epitomizes the music called jazz. May this token bring you luck for the rest of your life," I said. He was totally "gob smacked." I told him that one of my theories of life was that some items of great sentimental value have to be passed on, in special circumstances, to another who would appreciate it equally. This was that time, and he was the one I had chosen to receive this item and hopefully to keep it for the next twenty years just as I had done.

I could not close this chapter without mentioning two King Street boys who have worked so hard to keep jazz alive in my hometown of Pontypool. Their involvement in the local music scene has made the Jazz in the Park Festival a huge successful accomplishment, and I wish continued good fortune to Tom and Brian Williams.

Thirty One
The Memories

Just recently I switched on to a British sports channel on my television at home, and there, peering back at me, was Trevor Francis, a long lost acquaintance of mine. The first time I saw Trevor was in America at his initial game for the Detroit Express Soccer Club at Pontiac Silverdome, and in American style it was different.

All the players from both teams lined up facing each other, about ten yards apart, in the middle of the field and then with an entrance that only the Yanks can do, Trevor appeared. With a fanfare of music and a multitude of spotlights, onto the field came a white convertible, chauffeur-driven, Rolls Royce sedan. It stopped on the center spot of the soccer field and out stepped Trevor in all his glory. The newspapers had been heralding his arrival for several weeks prior, and so there were about twenty thousand fans all going crazy as he exited his ride. They would not be disappointed. That night the Express beat a star-studded New York Cosmos team by eight goals to one and Trevor Francis scored six of them. He was in a class above everyone else as with great speed he effortlessly glided past opponents as if they were shadows on the ground. In the Main Event Restaurant after the game, I shook his hand for the first time of what was to become a regular occurrence thereafter. At the end of that season, Detroit

Express went down to Tampa Bay (near where I now live) to play the Rowdies in the National Soccer League Cup play-offs. They were beaten in extra time, so Rodney Marsh and his boys had the last laugh. A group of us ardent fans were so proud of our team that we were all at Detroit Metro Airport at 2:00 a.m. when the team arrived back. Most of us had actually watched the game live on television, but even with a loss we were overjoyed with our team's achievements. I singled out Trevor and cornered him to get his views on the game and the performance of the team. His exact words to me were, "If the goalpost would have been round and not square, Detroit would have won in regulation time." I knew what he meant, because I had witnessed the event on television, where he'd run right through the opponents' defense and thundered a shot against the post with the goalkeeper beaten all ends up. The ball hit the inside edge of the square post and cannoned back out; if the post had been round, the ball would have deflected into the net for a win. Trevor was obviously disappointed, but the fans would hear none of this, because they were so pleased to have such a class act as Trevor on and off the field of play.

The last time I spoke with Trevor Francis was not a happy occasion for two reasons. One was that his contract had finished with the Express, and he was to return to England. The second reason, which was even more serious, was that he had a broken cheekbone picked up from an opponent's flying elbow. Trevor had already played for England in the 1982 World Cup in Spain but this injury proved bad enough to keep him out of the 1986 World Cup in Mexico. This was a shame because on merit he deserved to be there and add more glory to his illustrious career. Apart from the Detroit Express, he had also played for his hometown team, Birmingham City, from the age of sixteen. He then joined Nottingham Forest and won two European Cup Finals under Manager Brian Clough. This transfer happened in 1979 when Trevor became the first player in the World to change clubs for £1 million.

He then went to Italy and played for Sampdoria and Atalanta before returning to England and playing for Manchester City, Glasgow Rangers, and finally Queens Park Rangers in London. He represented England fifty-two times. Trevor hung up his boots at the end of the 1988-89 season as one of the most prolific goal scorers of his time. Not only was he a great player, he was a gentleman in every respect.

In my office at my home on Anna Maria Island, I have many photographs of the teams that I have played for and some of the inspirational people whom I have played with or met. One of my personal favorite photographs is of Trevor, Debbie Harrison (as she was known then), and me. It is in the middle of one of those collage-type picture frames and I look at it often and remember those happy times. Trevor has since tried his hand at managing soccer teams at the highest level in England but has now moved on to become a television soccer match commentator. He now has the touches of gray in his hair that we all get in our later days, but he is still the class act that he always was. If I could pick a soccer team out of the star players that I have personally met, he would be one of my first choices. In fact the team would be as follows:

George Best (Northern Ireland), Trevor Francis (England), Jimmy Johnstone (Scotland), Paul Mariner (England), Carlos Valdarama (Columbia), Mike England (Wales), Bobby Moore (England), Alan Ball (England), Billy Bonds (England), Emlyn Hughes (England,) and Jim Brown (Scotland) goalkeeper. Reserves Rodney Marsh (England), Ian Callaghan (England), Steve Heighway (Ireland), and Mark Hately (England).

Of course some of them would have to play out of position. Perhaps even Rod Stewart would like to go on for a spell because he could have been a professional soccer player but for the fact that he chose music as his life's work instead.

Around the same time, after one of the Detroit Express

home games at the Pontiac Silverdome, I was invited to go to a nightclub with some of the players. As I remember, there was Brian Tinnion, Gus Moffat, Davie Bradford, Steve Seargent, Alan Brasil, Mark Hately, and me (all Brits you'll notice). I took off to bring my car over from the parking lot to the front of the Main Event Restaurant so we could make a quick getaway as soon as the post-game reception was over. About an hour later, the party ended, and we all made a hurried exit so that we could move on to the next watering hole without delay. Alas, when we arrived at my car I found I had accidentally locked my keys inside the car. From the driver's side window I could see them dangling from the ignition. What a bummer! We tried all sorts of things to get into the car but to no avail. Someone even went back into the restaurant and returned with a wire coat hanger and, as a last resort, we individually tried to slip the catch on the driver's door lock but once again, no luck. I was giving it one last try, and as I struggled with the lock, I happened to look up and see Davie Bradford grinning at me while leaning through the passenger side window, which had been wide open all the time. If it had been partially open it could easily have been seen but being totally open it looked exactly the same as being totally closed except for no glass. Once again the lunatics were running the asylum.

During this period, Brian Tinnion and Gus Moffat were partners with me when I initially opened my soccer supply store but they were also playing for the Detroit Express. To keep their anonymity, we named the business Metro Tri County Soccer Supply but the M. T. C. was really Moffat, Tinnion and Clarke. They were able to funnel a good amount of business from the Express Soccer Camps through our company, which I exclusively ran. This was all done with great secrecy because this was a conflict of interest and if found out could have jeopardized their professional careers with the Express and the National Soccer League. They did not take money from the company on a regular basis but instead took it at times of need.

One day they both came to me to say that the Express could not pay them because the owner had a financial problem. This was a few weeks before Christmas and they both needed cash badly, so we sat down and thrashed out a payment that was fair and equitable to all concerned. It was further agreed that this payment to them would constitute a buyout and that henceforth they were no longer partners of M.T.C. Soccer Supply. We still remained friends, and they still channeled business in my direction from their many contacts. As the saying goes, "If winning is not important, why bother to keep score?"

Thirty Two
The Summation

As I sit here looking back over the years, my memories are so vivid! I have seen and met some of the finest players in the world of rugby, soccer, tennis, athletics, ice hockey, and American football. I have been to the Indy 500 Speedway Race and experienced the sheer power of the cars as they thundered past me. I have enjoyed the thrill of horse racing (the sport of kings) at Epsom and Sandown race courses, the excitement being enhanced by a "flutter on the gee-gees." I have attended the Grand National at Aintree and witnessed Red Rum's historic victories. I have entertained customers on a 130-foot company yacht and slept in the captain's quarters. In fact, I've spent time on that very same yacht in Detroit, Bay City, Chicago, Peoria, and St. Louis. I have experienced the buzz of the World Soccer Cup in 1994 and the World Rugby Cup in 1999. I have enjoyed the Formula One Grand Prix, the cars racing through the streets of Detroit, and at a later time, the same event held on Belle Isle in the middle of the Detroit River. I have been to championship boxing, where I saw Howard Winstone defending his world title at Liverpool. I have been involved in international yacht racing and met some of the most talented sailors from around the world — —bar none.

I have partied on Church Street, Liverpool; on Beale Street, Memphis, Tennessee; on Bourbon Street, New Orleans; on Duval Street, Key West; and on Fremont Street, Las Vegas. I have rubbed shoulders with some of the most interesting, influential, and wealthiest people on planet Earth. I have done the Spanish, French, and Italian Rivieras. I have swum in the Mediterranean and Caribbean Seas and also the Gulf of Mexico. I have visited ancient ruins in the jungles of Central America. I have toured Sweden, Germany, Switzerland, Spain, Italy, and France. I have visited two-thirds of the U.S. mainland. I have been to stage musical shows, live music concerts and festivals, and, of course, nightclubs. I've enjoyed all sorts of music from classical to rock, country, soul, Bluegrass, jazz, and pure blues. I have played rugby, soccer, tennis, pool, and athletics and have achieved a reasonable level of proficiency in all of them. I have loved and been loved by some of the kindest, warmest, fun-loving women around — — but none better than my present wife, Sharon, without whose love I would be like a rudderless ship adrift at sea.

Apart from my regular daily jobs, I have always had additional ways of making money. At the age of eighteen, I was a bookie's runner, personally covering any bets that I thought had no chance of winning. All other bets were passed on through to the bookie. On several occasions, I've acted as an independent salesman for various small engineering companies that paid me cash commission on any work I sent their way. I did this back in the UK, and I did it here in America. I was the owner of my own small distribution company, selling industrial-strength liquid cleaner all over the Merseyside region. I've run a lottery syndicate with members paying me money to select the lottery numbers and buy all the tickets for them. I've owned three sporting goods stores specializing mainly in soccer, rugby, and Gaelic football but also involving other leisure activities. From this, I developed a mail-order company supplying European soccer and rugby merchandise (at an increased rate of profit) because I had a specialized niche clientele.

To this very day, I still search the For Sale and Wanted ads and am continually buying and selling various items from sports equipment and wear, to military badges, china pieces, various books, autographs, and assorted memorabilia. At the moment, I own a number of payphones. I have these located in the poorer sections of towns where, even today, they are used quite extensively. This current venture of mine has not yet recouped my initial investment, but I'll keep hacking away until I'm free and clear of my outlay. Then I'll be able to just empty the phones of the cash and laugh all the way to the bank.

Going to a thrift store, picking up an item for, say, five dollars, and then selling it to someone for twenty dollars, is something that I just can't get out of my system. Nothing beats dealing in cash! I have always found that paying people in hard cash always brings a favorable outcome by way of a discounted price or some extras thrown in at no additional cost. Of course, this is why barrow boys, street vendors, and the like always have more money than people think. This is because no one can keep tabs on how much they earn, and the honor system never works for those with no honor.

I have also had some hilarious moments working with some of the craziest people around. One night, I slipped a small, dead tropical fish into a friend's drink; and not noticing, he downed it without missing a beat. The "fish drinker," my friend John Cooper, was leaving Merseyside to go back to South Wales, and I'm sure that anyone who attended that function will never forget that incident. Any function I attended after that, everyone kept an eye on their drinks, just in case there was to be a repetition of the dead fish drop.

On another occasion I was in a beer garden in Hanover (Germany) with a crazy guy named Derek Gould. He climbed up onto the stage while the oompah band was taking a break and poured a whole stein of lager into one of the saxophones left on its stand. When the band returned and began to play, the saxophonist couldn't get any sound out of his instrument. He automatically lifted the instrument into the air and turned it upside down, peering into the bowl. Naturally, he received a deluge of beer all over his head. Derek and I laughed so hard, we gave the game away and were soon dragged, kicking and screaming from the table, and thrown out into the street. You can't replace moments like that!

At Girling Ltd. (Bromborough) the production managers requested that we methods engineers be put on the night shift to cover any potential problems that might arise and which would normally have to wait until the morning shift to be put right. We had six engineers, so it was decided that three would work on the day shifts, and the other three would work on nights. This would alternate on a weekly basis, one week of days, then one week of nights. Pretty soon, we got fed up with the night shift, so we devised a plan where one engineer would stay on duty while the other two would disappear into the night. The one left would clock the other two off at the end of the night shift and also cover for them during the night.

One night Joe Enwright and I decided to go clubbing over in Liverpool. We were driving along Dale Street when two girls waved us down. As Joe swung the car toward the curb (sidewalk), one of the girls stepped off into the road in anticipation of a lift. As bad luck would have it, Joe ran right over her foot. The night air was now blue with obscenities, and when Joe asked me if he should back up to see how the girl was, I advised him to keep going else "the beastie would devour us both!" God, those night shifts were killers!

One night in Omaha, Nebraska, after a hard day at an engineering exhibition, we congregated at the bar of the Holiday Inn. A large group of ladies were sitting near us, and as a guy arrived to take one of them home, he sat at their table for a moment. One of the ladies, with a very large pair of bosoms and the number ninety-nine on her tee shirt, sneaked up behind this guy, raised her shirt, and pulled it over his head. It was an extremely funny incident, and still laughing at it, I excused myself to visit the men's room. On my return, we moved from the bar to a nearby table, and within minutes of my sitting down, my head was suddenly enveloped in a very large tee shirt with two enormous "melons" pressing against my ears. Yes, this time the laugh was on me!

The Conclusion

I have not revealed all of the remarkable situations and events that I have experienced. My wandering mind finds it difficult to put them all into chronological order. Only when I witness an event or hear a story do I get flashbacks which bring memories to surface. Rather than overload the memory, I would rather save these additional stories for another time, perhaps the second exposé.

My aim has been to give you, the reader, some kind of insight into the wild and crazy life that I have lived. As I said at the beginning, many of the people I know from Wales and England have absolutely no idea of what my life in America has been like. Nor do my friends in the U.S. have any idea about my previous life and times in the old country.

If some of my antics have brought a smile to one's lips or have conjured up a memory from the past, then I'm happy. Perhaps because I'm approaching the twilight of my years and have thought long and hard about my beginnings, my journey along the way, and the place in which I now live, I have been compelled to tell this collection of anecdotes.

Every day that I wake up I think, in the words of Jimmy Buffett, "Another Day in Paradise," and my life is now as near to perfection as any life that I can imagine anyone experiencing.

I'm nowhere near a millionaire, but I live comfortably and have good health and sun on my back for almost 365 days of the year. Rubbing shoulders with happy, carefree people who have achieved their life's ambition by opting out of the rat race makes my life even more pleasant.

When I ponder on my chance meeting with Ray Milland all those years ago, I wonder how my life would have been without that encounter. Those twenty minutes changed my life forever, and if he were alive today, I would thank him enormously. Perhaps he would be pleased that he taught a young Pontypool boy what life is really about. God bless the Rajah!

Disclaimer

I have talked a lot about Ray Milland and his association with my home town of Pontypool. Ray did live there for a short time, staying with his cousin, but I am well aware that he was born and raised in the little town of Cymla, near Neath, South Wales. Incidentally, Ray Milland, my mother, and I all share the same birthday — —January 3.

Epilogue

Apart from those celebrities of the music industry mentioned in my book, I have also seen live, in concert, the following stars:

In England:

Buddy Holly, Sarah Vaughan, Ella Fitzgerald, Oscar Peterson, Sammy Davis, Jr., Ronnie Scott, the Ted Heath Orchestra, the Johnny Dankworth Band, Cleo Lane, the Eric Delaney Band, the Count Basie Orchestra, the Duke Ellington Band, Johnny Mathis, Shirley Bassie, Matt Monroe, Billy J. Kramer, Little Richard, the Stan Kenton Orchestra, the Gerry Mulligan Band, Thelonius Monk and the Modern Jazz Quartet, Freddie and the Dreamers, Rory Storm and the Hurricanes, Sophie Tucker, Mel Torme, Tommy Steele, and the Dave Bruebeck Quartet with Paul Desmond.

In America:

Neil Diamond, Chubby Checker, Gladys Knight and the Pips, Rich Little, Boy George, Christopher Cross, Howard Jones, Enrigue Iglesias, B.B. King, Cherry Popping Daddies, the Who, Gary Glitter, Billy Fury, Keb Moe, Bonny Raitt,

Paul Simon, Bob Dylan, Seanad O'Connor, Alanis Morissette, Sarah McLachlan, Annie Lennox, Sting, and Aaron Neville and the Neville Brothers Band.

I have also seen the following live musical shows:

West Side Story, Cats, Evita, Miss Saigon, Lord of the Dance (with Michael Flatly), River Dance, Phantom of the Opera, and Les Miserables.

Apart from the sports celebrities mentioned in my book, I have personally met the following stars:

Rugby: From the 1970s (the golden age of Welsh rugby)

Bobby Windsor, Tony "Charlie" Faulkner, Geoff Wheel, Terry Cobner, Jeff Squires, Keith Jarrett, Eddie Butler, and John Jeffery, (all Welsh internationals)

From the 1980-1990s:

John Perkina, David Bishop, Kevin Moseley, Mark Brown, Stephen "Staff" Jones, Mark Ring, Mike "Spikey" Watkins, and Garin Jenkins, (all Welsh internationals).

Other internationals:

David Duckham (England), Eric Evans (England), John Carleton (England), Uiniati Moa (Tonga), and Sione Tu Ipuloti (Tonga).

From the current Welsh team:

Gareth Llewelynn, Michael Owen, Dafydd Jones, Gethin Jenkins, Huw Bennett, Duncan Jones, Martin Williams, Stephen Jones, and Adam Jones.

Soccer:

Emlyn Hughes, Ray Clements, Phil Thompson, Tony Creswell, Steve Hardwick, and Mike English.

Others:

Arnold Schwarzenegger (bodybuilder), Vinnie Johnson (basketball), Freddie Truman (cricketer), Brendan Foster (athletics), Marcel Dionne (ice hockey), Les Dawson (comedian), Kevin Glover (American football), Glenda Jackson (actress), and Elton John (musician extraordinaire). I was also in the same reception room as the Rolling Stones, but the dense crowd prevented me from meeting them.

I have also, just recently, become an American citizen, which has added a further dimension to my checkered life.

Solitude

On Sabbath Day, far from the host,
To seek some solitude,
Up mountain shrouded, like a ghost,
By winding foot-path crude,
Climb to the top, passed fence and farm,
Over stiles, cross brook by stone,
My soul is captured with its calm,
The world and me alone,
At my favorite haunt I lie,
To nature I retreat,
The silence only broken by,
My heart's still pounding beat,
With eyes closed tight my ears detect,
Some single far off sound,
My senses now alert reflect,
Nature's beauty all around,
From the valley peals the sound of bells,
To add to all this bliss,
The soil's rich freshness softly smells,
And I will cherish this.

The Photo Album

Lyn, Taken At Nine Years Old

The James Gang

*Lyn, Sister Ann, Mother, &
Brother Chris*

The James Dean Look

Bullfighting in San Sebastian, 1960

*Lyn With Mom
At Darts Banquet.*

*Lyn Meeting An American
Indian.*

Lyn Relaxes Cowboy Style.

*Richard's First Cross
Country Race.*

Lyn With Daughter Louise.

Lyn's Son Richard With
Louise "Wham Kids"

Lyn At Abersoch.

Abersychan Tech Undefeated Rugby Team

Girling Apprentices - Newport Junior Cup Winners

Port Sunlight Team At The Isle Of Mann.

Port Sunlight Team,
Including Four County Players

Lucas Merseyside -
Seven-a-Side
Cup Winners

Lyn, Accepting Best Athlete
Award.

*Lyn Accepting Director's
Trophy For Best Team .*

Lucas Merseyside

*Lyn Taking A Kick For
Lucas Merseyside .*

Girling Apprentices, Soccer Champions.

Englishman gets kicks from soccer

By LeAnne Rogers
staff writer

When Lyn Clarke arrived in the United States from England 13 years ago, he rarely saw anyone playing soccer.

"Today you see soccer everywhere," the new Garden City business man said. "There is a terrific amount of soccer players in this area. There are probably 1,200 kids who play soccer in Livonia and 1,000 in Canton."

Growing up in Pontypool, Wales, Clarke grew up playing soccer during the week and rugby on the weekends.

It was his love of soccer which led him to open Metro Tri County Soccer Supply seven years ago. About a year ago, he moved MTC from its original Dearborn location to Ford just east of Middlebelt in Garden City.

"I was on the eastern edge of the youth soccer leagues, and I wanted to come further west," Clarke said. "I am better situated here. I get more walk in business and I draw customers from a wider area."

While the store carries some football shoes and some rugby equipment about 70 percent of the store's merchandise is soccer equipment and paraphernalia such as pins and posters.

"I stick with what I know," Clarke said. "There are so many stores with ski equipment and tennis equipment. It's best to stay with what you know and where you have contacts."

National soccer industry figures show the sport as second only to basketball among youngsters under 12 and third for teenagers up to 18 years, according to Clarke.

"HAVING THE soccer games on cable television really helped and the coaching has really improved," he said. "It was a shame before because American kids didn't see the standard of play elsewhere."

Still an active player, Clarke has coached youth and adult teams. He was founder and president of the Great Lakes Men's Soccer League until 1984.

These days Clarke said his customers look for soccer shirts of their favorite teams, soccer pins and posters of favorite players.

Efforts to promote soccer about 10 years ago were based on introducing big name foreign soccer players to American teams. That idea didn't work, Clarke said, but the sport gained popularity when grass roots instruction was implemented.

Please turn to Page 2

ART EMANUELE/staff photographs
Lyn Clarke shows off an Italian soccer team shirt at his Metro Tri County Soccer Supply business.

Englishman's favorite sport changed his life

Continued from Page 1

"This was one of the last areas in the U.S. to really get into soccer," he added. "You'd see a lot of it in places like Texas or Chicago."

THE POPULARITY of soccer should continue to grow, Clarke said since the 1994 World Cup soccer championships will be held in this country for the first time.

"The host team automatically qualifies so the American team will be participating," he said. "They haven't determined a site yet but the University of Michigan stadium has been mentioned."

Since giving up his career in engineering two years ago, Clarke has devoted himself to running the store and a new mail order operation.

"I have been sending stuff all over the country," he said. "I get calls from a lot of parts of America where there isn't a soccer store within 100 miles."

While having a career in engineering, Clarke said soccer and music were his two loves. He said music was what attracted him to the move from Wales to Cheshire, near Liverpool, in the mid 1960s.

BRITISH PUBS close at 11 p.m. so one night Clarke said he and a friend tipped the doorman at the Pink Parrot club in Liverpool, which had entertainment, and was allowed to serve drinks to members after hours.

Clarke and his friend joined two other young men at the club's bar and bought them drinks as they chatted.

"You know how your eyes have to adjust when you go into some place dark," he said. "We were talking and my friend kept looking past me at these two guys."

At his friend's prodding, Clarke said he recognized the pair and realized he was talking to Paul McCartney and John Lennon.

"They were living in London then and just visiting Liverpool," he said. "McCartney kept talking away, but Lennon never said anything unless you asked a direct question. Then he'd answer with as few words as possible."

It is kind of ironic, Clarke said, that he ended up in the Detroit area where his other favorite music came from during the 1960s.

Lyn Gets Publicity. Unfortunately The Reporter Labeled Him As An Englishman

Lyn During Relay Races.

Lyn During Relay Races.

Girling Cwmbran Works Athletic Team, Decathalon Champs.

Girling Apprentices, Team Shield Winners.

*Lyn And Sharon Celebrate Their Wedding
At The Beach.*

*Lyn And Sharon's Favorite Bar -
"The Drift Inn", Anna Maria Island*

*Lyn On Bradenton Beach
With The Manatees.*

*Lyn And Sharon Outside
Their Florida Home.*

*Lyn And Wife Sharon (middle) With Friends
Sue And Wayne*

Lyn And Sharon With Mostyn Conner
And Mike Nute

Lyn And Sharon With
Friend.

Made in the USA
Charleston, SC
23 December 2011